PHANTASTIC:
The 2008 World Champion Philadelphia Phillies

Shane Victorino celebrates his two-run home run to tie the game in the 8th inning against the Los Angeles Dodgers in Game 4 of the National League Championship Series on October 13, 2008, in Los Angeles.

TRIUMPH
BOOKS

The Phillies and their fans celebrate after winning Game 5 of the
baseball World Series at home on Wednesday, October 29, 2008.
The Phillies defeated the Tampa Bay Rays 4–3 to win the World Series
in Game 5 after an epic two-day rain delay.

This book is available in quantity at special discounts for your group
or organization. For further information, contact:

Triumph Books
542 South Dearborn Street
Suite 750
Chicago, Illinois 60605
(312) 939-3330
Fax (312) 663-3557

Printed in United States of America
ISBN: 978-1-60078-250-3

Written by: Fran Zimniuch

Photos courtesy of AP Images

Content packaged by Mojo Media, Inc.
Joe Funk: Editor
Jason Hinman: Creative Director

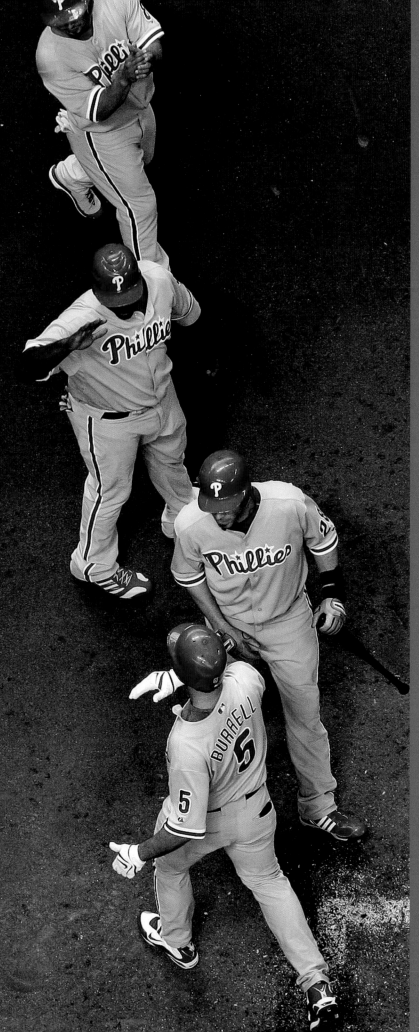

contents

Phillies players, from top to bottom, Shane Victorino, Ryan Howard, and Jayson Werth congratulate Pat Burrell after he hit a three-run home run in the third-inning of Game 4 of the National League Division Series against the Milwaukee Brewers on October 5, 2008, in Milwaukee.

Introduction

"Hard to believe, Harry!"

That would have no doubt been the cheerful refrain from the late, great Phillies icon Richie Ashburn, were he alive to see his favorite team reach the World Series in 2008. Ashburn, a Hall of Fame center fielder and broadcaster with the Phillies, passed away in 1997. But just about every Phillies fan considered "Whitey" their best friend. Thanks to his more than 30 years of broadcasting games, he was part of their family. People all across the region would often imitate Ashburn talking to his broadcasting partner Harry Kalas, to whom he'd often quip, "Hard to believe, Harry."

A World Series is hard to believe for Philadelphia baseball fans. They have supported the team since its inception in 1884, but along the way the Phillies have amassed the most losses of any pro sports' franchise— 10,101 compared to only 8,951 wins. Another way to look at this record is that the Phillies must have sported some pretty competitive teams to stay in business long enough to lose so many games. (Kind of a backhanded compliment, but it works.)

The 2008 Phillies thrilled their fans and energized an entire geographic region with yet another late-season surge to overtake the New York Mets, their dastardly division rivals 90 miles located north up the New Jersey Turnpike.

Charlie Manuel's team does it all. Cole Hamels and Jamie Moyer anchor a strong staff of starting pitchers. J.C. Romero, Chad Durbin, and Ryan Madson act as a bridge to Lidge— closer Brad Lidge who was perfect in 2008 converting 41 saves in 41 chances.

The Phillies can also hit. Ryan Howard had a monster year leading the league in home runs and runs batted in. Chase Utley, Pat Burrell, Jimmy Rollins, Shane Victorino, Jayson Werth, Greg Dobbs, and a host of others contributed mightily to the Phillies' cause this past season. No matter what the score, opposing teams could never count the Phillies out until the 27th out was made. And no matter what game, opposing teams never knew which Phillies player was going to beat them. It could be Hamels. It could be Brett Myers. It could be Howard. Or it could be backup catcher Chris Coste.

Citizen's Bank Park became the place for a modern-day baseball love-in as 3,422,583 fans filled the stadium during the season to cheer for their beloved Phightin' Phils. As the team clinched the division title and won two tough playoff series to gain entrance to baseball's Fall Classic, the stadium shook and fireworks lit the sky and a city and region celebrated en masse.

This 2008 Phillies team is just the sixth one in club history to get to the World Series. In 1915, 1950, 1983, and 1993, they came up short. But the glorious 1980 team of Dallas Green, Steve Carlton, Mike Schmidt, the late

Tug McGraw, and Pete Rose put Philadelphia baseball on the map as the ultimate winner. That team may have been the lone World Champion to grace the franchise up to now, but there were many teams over the past 30 seasons that came close.

Past playoff teams include those who won the East Division in 1976, 1977, 1978, 1980, 1983, 1993, and 2007. So while the franchise may have had some lean times over the years, there have also been a number of talented squads that have sparked interest in Philadelphia baseball even as the leaves were starting to turn color.

Through the years the Phillies have competed and come tantalizingly close on numerous occasions. The 1980 team won it all but the team has done its fans proud more often than not. And through it all, win or lose, Phillies fans continue to live and die with the team. That's why there is such genuine joy being felt about another trip to the World Series. When you consider the love and dedication that Phillies fans have for their team, 2008's championship run is a well-earned reward for more than a century of loyal support. ⦾

Tampa Bay Rays' B.J. Upton scores the tying run past Carlos Ruiz in the sixth inning of Game 5 of the World Series at Citizens Bank Park on October 27. The run would prolong Philadelphia's championship dry spell—for two more days.

We Win!!!

"We win," and "Phineally" were two of the more popular refrains as fans poured onto the streets of the Delaware Valley to celebrate the Philadelphia Phillies second World Series title in the team's 126-year history. When the final nasty slider of Brad Lidge's perfect 2008 season eluded Tampa Bay Rays pinch-hitter Eric Hinske with two out in the bottom of the ninth inning of Game 5, the Phillies long-awaited return to baseball's promised land had finally arrived thanks to a 4-3 victory.

In one of the strangest, weirdest, most off-the-wall World Series–deciding games in the history of baseball, a Pat Burrell double and a Pedro Feliz single plated what was ultimately to be the winning run in a four-games-to-one win for Philadelphia in the 2008 Fall Classic. While the World Series victory served to exorcise 28 years of demons that kept the Phillies from the title—and was the first Philadelphia professional-sport championship since the Sixers captured the NBA title in 1983—the fifth and deciding game of the Series will go down in infamy.

It took nearly 50 hours to complete Game 5. The contest started innocently enough on the evening of Monday October 27, with the Phillies opening up a quick 2-0 lead behind their ace left-hander Cole Hamels. But the weather conditions steadily worsened, with chilly temperatures soon joined by a strong rain storm that settled in for what promised to be a long stay. The sloppy field conditions—the kind that favor a "mudder" in horse racing—helped Tampa tie the game 2-2 in the top of the sixth inning.

With two outs, B.J. Upton slapped a sharp grounder to the left of Phils shortstop Jimmy Rollins that in normal conditions would probably have been a routine out. Instead, the ball skipped over Rollins' glove into left field for

Chase Utley get things started for a bang for the Phillies as he hits a two-run home run off Tampa Bay Rays starting pitcher Scott Kazmir in the first inning of Game 1 of the World Series in St. Petersburg, Florida on October 22, 2008.

The Phillies managed to split
the first two games, held at
the peculiar dome known as
Tropicana Field, the Rays' home.

what was ruled a single. The speedy Upton got a big jump on Hamels and easily stole second and Carlos Pena knocked him in with another single to left. Hamels retired the next batter, but the damage was done.

Much to the chagrin of Phillies fans, the umpires called the players off the field, which was then covered with a tarp by the hard-working grounds crew in the hope that the game might be continued after a delay. The weather didn't cooperate and the game was suspended for the night with the Phillies coming up to bat in the home half of the sixth inning.

A miserable Tuesday forecast that promised nothing but hard rain and cold temperatures prompted MLB to push the restart off even further. The best hope to resume the series appeared to be on Wednesday evening, which also offered less-than-ideal conditions: temperatures in the lower 40s with a wind chill in the upper 30s at Citizen's Bank Park. It was a bone-chilling cold evening, but at least it was dry and thanks to the work of the grounds crew at the ballpark, the field was in excellent condition. But after the two-day delay, what turned out to be the deciding game of the World Series amounted to a three-and-one-half-inning sprint to the finish.

In their first at bat in two days it didn't take the Phillies long to break the 2-2 tie. Geoff Jenkins, batting for pitcher Cole Hamels—who had pitched six strong innings two days before and was destined to be name the Series MVP—smashed a double to center field to lead off the home sixth. After Jimmy Rollins bunted Jenkins to third, the reserve outfielder scored on a bloop single to center field off the bat of

Jayson Werth. The Phillies were now up 3-2 with just nine outs separating them from their second championship.

Of course, it could never be that easy for a Phillies team. In the top of the seventh, Rocco Baldelli, the pride of Woonsocket, Rhode Island whose playing in 2008 had been limited by severe health problems, lined a Ryan Madson fastball into the left-field stands to tie the score at 3-3. After a two-day delay, could the fifth game be headed into extra innings, or even perhaps back to Tampa for the sixth and seventh games?

That prospect was not to be as the combination of Pat Burrell and Pedro Feliz responded in the home seventh to put the Phillies up 4-3 in front of a throng of cold but incredibly excited fans filling Citizen's Bank Park. One of the Phillies strengths for the entire season was the bullpen. Brad Lidge was "Lights Out Lidge" all season long, but the set-up crew that consisted of Madson, Chad Durbin, and J.C. Romero were money in the bank as well.

With their new-found lead and the championship within their grasp, the Phillies turned to Romero to pitch the eighth inning. The flame-throwing southpaw who had been outstanding all season long got through the inning without giving up a run. The Phillies failed to score in the home ninth, but they had their lead and were just three outs away from a World Series championship.

Much like 28 years before against the Kansas City Royals in 1980 when the closer out of the bullpen, the late Tug McGraw, was called in to shut down the Royals in the ninth

Cole Hamels was named MVP after his performance in the World Series.

World Series Stats

Game 1 • October 22, 2008, at Tropicana Field

	1	2	3	4	5	6	7	8	9	R	H	E
Philadelphia Phillies	2	0	0	1	0	0	0	0	0	3	8	1
Tampa Bay Rays	0	0	0	1	1	0	0	0	0	2	5	1

PITCHERS: PHI - Hamels, Madson (8), Lidge (9) • TBR - Kazmir, Howell (7), Balfour (7), Miller (9), Wheeler (9)
WP - Cole Hamels • LP - Scott Kazmir • SAVE - Brad Lidge
HOME RUNS: PHI - Utley • TBR - Crawford • **ATTENDANCE:** 40,783

Game 2 • October 23, 2008, at Tropicana Field

	1	2	3	4	5	6	7	8	9	R	H	E
Philadelphia Phillies	0	0	0	0	0	0	0	1	1	2	9	2
Tampa Bay Rays	2	1	0	1	0	0	0	0	x	4	7	1

PITCHERS: PHI - Myers, Romero (8) • TBR - Shields, Wheeler (6), Price (7) • WP - James Shields • LP - Brett Myers
SAVE - none
HOME RUNS: PHI - Bruntlett • TBR - none • **ATTENDANCE:** 40,843

Game 3 • October 25, 2008, at Citizens Bank Park

	1	2	3	4	5	6	7	8	9	R	H	E
Tampa Bay Rays	0	1	0	0	0	0	2	1	0	4	6	1
Philadelphia Phillies	1	1	0	0	0	2	0	0	1	5	7	1

PITCHERS: TBR - Garza, Bradford (7), Howell (8), Balfour (9) • PHI - Moyer, Durbin (7), Eyre (7), Madson (8), Romero (8)
WP - J.C. Romero • LP - J.P. Howell • SAVE - none
HOME RUNS: TBR - none • PHI - Howard, Ruiz, Utley • **ATTENDANCE:** 45,900

Game 4 • October 26, 2008, at Citizens Bank Park

	1	2	3	4	5	6	7	8	9	R	H	E
Tampa Bay Rays	0	0	0	1	1	0	0	0	0	2	5	2
Philadelphia Phillies	1	0	1	3	1	0	0	4	x	10	12	1

PITCHERS: TBR - Sonnanstine, Jackson (5), Wheeler (7), Miller (8) • PHI - Blanton, Durbin (7), Eyre (7), Madson (7),
Romero (9) • WP - Joe Blanton • LP - Andy Sonnanstine • SAVE - none
HOME RUNS: TBR - Crawford, Hinske • PHI - Blanton, Howard (2), Werth • **ATTENDANCE:** 45,903

Game 5 • October 27 & 29, 2008, at Citizens Bank Park

	1	2	3	4	5	6	7	8	9	R	H	E
Tampa Bay Rays	0	0	0	1	0	1	1	0	0	3	10	0
Philadelphia Phillies	2	0	0	0	0	1	1	0	x	4	8	1

PITCHERS: TBR - Kazmir, Balfour (5), Howell (6), Bradford (7), Price (8) • PHI - Hamels, Madson (7), Romero (8), Lidge (9)
WP - Romero • LP - Howell • SAVE - Lidge

inning, it was Brad Lidge-time in Philadelphia in 2008. The big, hard-throwing right-hander was acquired by the Phillies in an off-season trade with the Houston Astros. He was so impressively dominant after arriving in Philadelphia that the team signed him to a contract extension during the season. Lidge posted 41 saves in 41 save opportunities during the regular season and had followed with six more saves in six postseason opportunities. He was a perfect 47 for 47 in 2008 with the deciding game in his control in the ninth inning. He was the right man for the Phillies to have on the mound when just three outs separated them from a title.

The first batter for Tampa, rookie sensation Even Longoria, popped out to second baseman Chase Utley for the first out of the inning. But on an 0-2 pitch, catcher Dioner Navarro punched a broken-bat single to center field. Pinch runner Fernando Perez stole second base; he represented the tying run with just one out.

That's when Lidge went to work and induced pinch hitter Ben Zobrist to line out to Werth in right field for the second out of the inning. And finally at 10:01 pm on Wednesday, October 29, Lidge struck out pinch-hitter Eric Hinske on a nasty slider—reminiscent of how Tug McGraw fanned Willie Wilson 28 years before—and the Phillies were World Series champions.

The champagne was pouring and the players were enjoying their moment in the sun. But in the streets in neighborhoods across an entire region, tens of thousands of fans celebrated a long-awaited championship that finally belonged to Philadelphia. And the Phillies were the team to bring the title home.

"We win!"

"Phineally." ①

Carlos Ruiz tags out Jason Bartlett as he tries to score from second on a single by Akinori Iwamura during the seventh inning of Game 5.

Ryan Howard

What does Ryan Howard have in common with Jimmie Foxx, Hank Greenberg, and Mark McGwire? They are all tied for 10th place for the all-time single-season home run record of 58, behind only the likes of Barry Bonds, Sammy Sosa, Roger Maris, and George Herman "Babe" Ruth.

Ryan Howard came onto the scene in Philadelphia during the 2005 season with much the same effect as the Big Bang Theory. Just two years prior, popular power hitter Jim Thome of the Cleveland Indians had signed a big free-agent contract that promised to make him a fixture at first base for the Phillies for years to come. And Thome did not disappoint, slugging 89 homers and driving in 236 runs in 2003 and 2004. He was the toast of the town. But nagging injuries kept him out of all but 59 games in 2005, opening the door for the gentle giant, Ryan Howard.

A muscular 6-foot-4 and 256 pounds, Howard was originally selected by the Phillies in the fifth round of the draft in June 2001. In 2002 with Lakewood, in his first full minor-league season, Howard hit .280 with 19 homers and 87 RBIs. He put together a solid campaign the following season in Clearwater, slugging a league-leading 23 homers with 82 RBIs.

While Thome was making Phillies fans happy in 2004, Ryan Howard put together a monster minor league season. With impressive stops at Reading and Scranton before a September call-up by Philadelphia, Howard combined to hit 48 home runs and knock in 137 RBIs. Few realized at the time that the soft-spoken giant was about to put up those kind of numbers in the major leagues on a regular basis.

The 2005 season saw fate play its ultimate hand in the Phillies' first-base situation. Thome, coming off those two fantastic seasons, suffered an elbow injury that limited him just 59 largely ineffective games. That opened the door for Howard, who hit .288 with 22 homers and 63 RBIs, good enough to be named the National League's Rookie of the Year.

His success put Phillies management into a pleasantly difficult position. Even though the old axiom was that a player does not lose his job due to injury, Howard was younger, stronger, and even more dynamic a player than the popular Thome. Someone had to go. But who would it be? They could trade the veteran Thome and take a chance on the still largely untested Howard. Or deal the young stud of their organization who could conceivably put up even bigger numbers than Gentleman Jim for considerably more years.

"In 2007, Howard became the fastest player
to reach 100 home runs in major league history."

Some worried that trading Howard might haunt the organization for decades in the way that Ferguson Jenkins and Ryne Sandberg did after being dealt from Philadelphia.

The Phillies ultimately chose the younger player and in November of 2005 dealt their biggest free agent signee, Jim Thome, to the Chicago White Sox in exchange for center fielder Aaron Rowand and pitchers Gio Gonzalez and Daniel Haigwood. The first base job now belonged solely to Ryan Howard and he was not about to disappoint.

If there is such a thing as the sophomore jinx in baseball, Howard is simply not a believer. While some players may have struggled with the pressure of replacing such a proven player and fan favorite as Jim Thome, all Howard did was prove day after day that the Phillies organization made the right decision. In his first full major-league season in 2006, Ryan Howard smacked 58 home runs, drove in 149 RBIs, and had a slugging percentage of .659. And as if that weren't enough, he hit a lofty .313 and earned the National League Most Valuable Player Award.

(Trivia: Who are the only two players to be voted Rookie of the Year and Most Valuable Player in consecutive seasons? Cal Ripken Jr. in 1982-83 and Ryan Howard in 2005-06.)

His gargantuan home runs and aw shucks persona made him an instant favorite with the fans and the press in the City of Brotherly Love. He also set an all-time major-league record for single-season home runs by a second-year player. His 58 dingers bested the likes of Ralph Kiner's 51, Eddie Matthews' 47, Joe DiMaggio's 46, and Jim Gentile's 46. His 149 RBIs as a sophomore in the major leagues was second all time to DiMaggio's 167 and ahead of Chuck Klein's 145.

As if that wasn't enough, Howard got national acclaim by winning the Home Run Derby at the All-Star Game in Pittsburgh on July 10.

Howard's second full season in the major leagues, 2007, saw him continue to be a dominant force in the Philadelphia lineup. While his average dipped to .268, he still smacked 47 home runs and drove in 136 runs. He spent 15 days on the disabled list in May due to a quadriceps strain, but came back strong after a brief rehab assignment. And one of his prouder moments occurred on August 21 against Los Angeles when he had his first career stolen base. Howard also grabbed another impressive record that season by becoming the fastest player to reach 100 home runs in major-league history.

While opposing left-handed pitchers could give the big first sacker a difficult time, after a slump he always seemed to be able to right himself. The strikeouts would always be there as he set a new major league record with 199. But he was a solid performer who helped the Phillies reach the post-season after many years' absence and he supported the team in its losing effort with a playoffs' home run against Colorado's Jeremy Affeldt.

As the Phillies successfully defended their division crown in 2008, Ryan Howard endured in many ways the most difficult year of his young career. After being awarded a $10 million salary in arbitration, he got off to a horrible start, hitting just .205 by the end of May. But to his credit, Howard worked through his early season struggles and the challenges of hitting left-handed pitching to end the season with a respectable .251 average. More importantly, he tallied an impressive 48 home runs and 146 RBIs, helping the Phillies to their second consecutive division crown. Ⓘ

Pat Burrell

Most baseball fans enjoy watching a slugger at the plate—the type of player who hits baseballs far enough and high enough to make it rain, while driving in around 100 runs per year. He may not always hit for a high average, but his hits normally mean something. Most franchises have a history of such sluggers and the Philadelphia Phillies are no different. Just some of their more famous power hitters from the right side of the plate include the likes of Del Ennis, Richie Allen, Greg Luzinski, and Hall of Famer Mike Schmidt.

There is no doubt that before a pair of long-ball-hitting lefties, Jim Thome and Ryan Howard, came to town, the next member of the dinger club was prototypical slugger Pat Burrell. He enjoyed an outstanding collegiate career at the University of Miami. In fact, Burrell was named Most Valuable Player in the 1996 College World Series. In his three years at Miami he hit .442, seventh on the all-time NCAA list, with 61 homers and 187 RBIs. Burrell's .888 slugging percentage was second all-time in NCAA history behind Oklahoma State's Pete Incaviglia, with .915.

After putting up such impressive numbers, there was little doubt he'd be a very high draft pick—which he was when the Phillies called his name in the first round of the 1998 Amateur Draft. Phillies fans and front office personnel alike breathed a huge sigh of relief that July when Burrell signed with the club. The Phillies' top pick in 1997, J.D. Drew, refused to sign with the club and was drafted and later signed by St. Louis in 1998. To this day, Drew is greeted with venom by Philadelphia fans who will never forgive him for his refusal to sign with the team. Behind closed doors, management does not necessarily belong to Drew's fan club either.

In his first full year of professional ball in 1999, Pat Burrell made his mark at Double A Reading, hitting .333 with 28 homers and 90 RBI's in 117 games. Needless to say, all of baseball sat up and took notice of this top-level prospect. After getting off to a good start with Scranton-Wilkes Barre in 2000, Burrell was recalled by Philadelphia and began what has been a steady, occasionally spectacular, career as the Phillies everyday left fielder.

He hit 18 homers and drove in 79 runs in his rookie year while boasting a .260 average. The following year saw steady improvement with 27 dingers and 89 RBIs, which was a nice prelude to his breakout season of 2002. That was the year that Burrell hit his career-high 37 homers while driving in 116 runs with a career-best .282 average. His only Achilles

"Burrell batted .250 and slugged 33 home runs while driving in 86 RBIs for the Phillies in 2008."

heel was his propensity for striking out. Burrell fanned 153 times in 586 at bats. But when a player hits the ball as far as he does as often as he does, strikeouts are a reasonable trade-off.

The young star in the making was blessed with movie-star good looks on his powerful 6-foot-4 inch, 235-pound frame. Coming off such a strong season in 2002, expectations were sky high in 2003. But Burrell suffered through what was his worst season in the majors, slumping to a frustrating .209 average with 21 homers and just 64 RBIs. He continued to strike out often and had become a focal point of some of the frustrations of the always-demanding Philadelphia fans. But Burrell refused to make excuses or bristle at the treatment he received from the fans. If anything, he even increased his incredible work ethic to snap out of his season-long slump.

Burrell rebounded to more typical numbers in 2004, but really returned to form in 2005 when he once again eclipsed the 30-homer mark with 32, while driving home a career -high 117 runs and posting a fine .281 average. While Burrell seemingly had gotten back to his regular production, the Phillies had become the bridesmaids of the National League, just not quite good enough to reach post-season play.

Charlie Manuel had replaced Larry Bowa at the helm of the team in 2005, but the team still finished in second place. The team had the same near miss in 2006 when Pat the Bat hit a respectable .258 with 29 homers and 95 RBIs. But years of Philly frustration were soon to end.

Finally in 2007, the Phillies were a team of destiny that would reach the playoffs for the first time since 1993 thanks to an incredible late-season surge and a New York Mets choke for the ages. Burrell hit .256 with 30 homers and 97 RBIs to help the team reach the playoffs. A player who has steadily gained favor from Phillies fans, Burrell showed his true colors as the ultimate team player with his celebratory charge from the dugout to congratulate pitcher Brett Myers after the final out of the playoff-clinching game. The normally slow-footed outfielder even beat catcher Chris Coste to the mound to congratulate Myers. While the Phils were swept by a white-hot Colorado Rockies team in the National League Division Series, they had finally gotten over that post-season hump.

Burrell's genuine joy over the playoff appearance allowed fans to see deeper than the unemotional, businesslike demeanor that he normally exhibits on the field. Fans even learned of the playful side of Burrell, who has mastered the art of flicking bottle caps with amazing accuracy.

As he entered the final year of the six-year contract extension he signed in 2003, Pat the Bat seemed intent on forcing the team to re-sign him. Off to a fantastic start, the big left fielder literally carried the Phillies through the first half of the 2008 season.

While he slumped in the second half of the season, Burrell still helped the team to its second consecutive division title with a .250 average, while slugging 33 homers and driving in 86 runs.

No matter whether he remains a member of the Phillies organization or moves on in 2009, Pat Burrell gave the team and city nine outstanding seasons.

26

Chase Utley

After Ryan Howard copped National League MVP honors in 2006 and Jimmy Rollins did the trick in 2007, there was hope and expectation in the Philadelphia area that second baseman Chase Utley would complete a three-pete in 2008. While the left-handed-hitting three-time All-Star had a stellar season with a .292 average, 33 homers, and 104 RBIs, those numbers will not get him serious MVP consideration.

But Utley certainly will get recognition as one of the top players in baseball and as one of the team leaders on the Phillies squad. Since taking over the second base spot from Placido Polanco early in the 2005 campaign, Utley has been at the top of a group of fine second sackers. In 2005 and 2006, he outhomered all other big league second basemen with 57 blasts. Craig Biggio was second with 47. He also led in RBIs at his position during the same time frame with 197, compared to his nearest competitor, Jeff Kent with 161. In short, Chase Utley is the real deal.

Utley made a name for himself in college at UCLA, where he hit .342. In his junior year with the Bruins, he hit the ball at a .382 clip, adding 22 home runs and 69 RBIs. He ranks fourth on UCLA's all-time home run list. Considering that he put up such numbers at

a very good athletic institution, it came as no surprise when he was chosen in the first round (15th overall) of the draft in 2000.

Breaking into pro ball that summer with the Batavia Muckdogs, Utley quickly climbed the ladder through the Phillies farm system, hitting .257 for Clearwater in 2001 and .263 with Scranton-Wilkes Barre in 2002 where he also hit a league-leading 39 doubles. The 2003 season saw him put together a solid year at Scranton as evidence by his .323 average. He also had a taste of the big leagues, hitting .239 in 43 games. In his first start in the majors, Utley hit a grand slam home run.

Utley spent most of the 2004 season with the Phillies, sharing time with Palanco and hitting .266 with 13 homers and 57 RBIs. As time wore on, he began to show that he could hit left-handed pitching, which enabled the organization to trade Polanco to Detroit in June of 2005 in exchange for reliever Ugueth Urbina and utility man Ramon Martinez. Given full reign at second base, Utley did not disappoint. At the same time many fans lament management's decision to trade Polanco, who has played extremely well for the Tigers. There was a school of thought that he should have been moved to third base to replace David Bell. But management felt that

"Utley had such a stellar season in 2008 that many thought he might be a candidate for MVP."

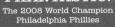

the addition of Urbina, a former closer, was worth the price.

After the Polanco trade, Chase Utley burst onto the scene as an everyday ballplayer and never looked back, hitting .291 with 28 homers and 105 RBIs. Not just an offensive weapon, he and shortstop Rollins have formed one of the most dependable double-play combinations in the game. With each ensuing season, Chase Utley appears to ramp up his game more and more. Such was the case in 2006 when he eclipsed the .300 mark for the first time in the major leagues with a .309 average, adding 32 homers and 102 RBIs. He gained national notoriety that year when he enjoyed a 35-game hitting streak, which was second in team history to Rollins, who had struck hits in 38 consecutive games.

He also played for Team USA in the World Baseball Classic, gaining instant national recognition.

Prior to the start of the 2007 season, Utley married and signed an $86 million contract that would partner he and the Phillies for another seven seasons. He responded with his best batting average, .332. And while he still added 22 home runs and 103 RBIs during the season, it could well be that his production suffered as a result of breaking a bone in his right hand when he was hit by a pitch thrown by John Lannan of the Washington Nationals. He spent some time on the disabled list and returned with a three-hit game, but the missed time and hand injury surely cost him some power numbers. But still, the Phillies earned their first playoff berth, albeit a short one.

That playoff experience certainly aided the team in 2008 as they were either in first or second place for much of the season. For his part, Utley got off to a red-hot start this season. He hit homers in five consecutive games during the first month of the season, tying a team record held by Dick Allen, Mike Schmidt, and Bobby Abreu. But for the first time in his career, Utley suffered through a slump that extended to one hit in 29 at-bats.

But he still hit well, hit in the clutch, and appeared in 159 games. The slump and a tail off in his power numbers during the last couple months of the season led to speculation that he might be playing with an injury. Regardless, he had another outstanding season and at the age of 29 gives the hope that many of his best years are still ahead of him.

Chase Utley may not have completed the third leg of the Phillies MVP awards in 2008, but anyone who has seen his determined style of play and his talent level knows that there is a good chance that the award will be in his future. ⊘

Jimmy Rollins

Some leaders on a baseball team do so by example on the playing field. Others work behind the scenes in the clubhouse to rally and encourage the troops. And yet another group of leaders are the ones who are the focal point with the press and the fans, acting as the voice of the team. In 2007 National League Most Valuable Player Jimmy Rollins the Phillies have a little bit of all three types.

"J-Roll," as he has become known in the Delaware Valley, led and willed the Phillies to the playoffs in 2007, garnering MVP honors. But as the team attempted to repeat its first-place finish in 2008, Rollins looked to maintain the same level of play that earned the three-time All-Star so many accolades. While the Phillies successfully defended their title and ultimately advanced to the World Series, 2008 was a bit of a struggle for Rollins. Considering the numbers he put up, to call his year a struggle is a testament to his ability.

Rollins' season may have been previewed when he sprained his ankle sliding back into second base trying to avoid a pick-off throw in April. After trying to play through the injury, he visited a place he had never been to before in his professional career—the 15-day disabled list. He returned to the lineup and reclaimed his spot at shortstop for rest of the season, hitting

.277 with 11 home runs and 59 RBIs. Those figures pale in comparison to his 2007 stats, which included a .296 average with 30 homers and 94 RBIs. But he played in 25 fewer games in 2008 and still stole more bases, got more walks, and had a higher on-base percentage than his MVP season. Even in what for him has been a sub-par year, he served the Phillies admirably as the prototypical leadoff hitter.

The switch-hitting, smooth-fielding short-stop was drafted by the Phillies in the second round of the 1996 amateur draft. In his first full season as a pro with the Class A Piedmont Boll Weevils in 1997, he hit .270 with six homers and 46 stolen bases. The following year with the Clearwater Phillies of the Florida State League, he hit just .244 with 23 steals on a team that included future big-league teammates Pat Burrell, Johnny Estrada, Adam Eaton, and Brandon Duckworth. He had been the youngest player of that team, but J-Roll got his career in gear in 1999 with the Double A Reading Phillies as he hit .273 with 11 homers, 56 RBI's and 24 steals. He led the team in games played, at-bats, and hits.

Rollins made the jump to Triple A Scranton-Wilkes Barre in 2000 and brought in the new millennium with style. Boasting a .274 batting average, he tied for the league lead in triples

"The switch-hitting, smooth-fielding, fast-running
Rollins was drafted by the Phillies in the second
round of the 1996 amateur draft."

with 11, knocked 12 homers, drove in 69 runs, and swiped 24 bases. By all accounts, he was ready for the major leagues in September when clubs expanded their rosters. The Phillies brought him up, and in his first major league month J-Roll hit .321 in 14 games. One look at the way he played the position indicated beyond the shadow of a doubt that the Phillies had found their shortstop of the future.

In his rookie season of 2001 Rollins made quite a splash. All he did was field his position flawlessly and use his speed and determination to hit a solid .274 with 14 homers and 54 RBIs. But in addition he led the league in at bats (656) and triples (12) and tied for the league lead in stolen bases with 46. Not surprisingly, he represented the Phillies in the midseason All-Star Game.

The following season Rollins again led the league with 637 at bats and 10 triples. And while his average tailed off to .245, defensively he had a .980 fielding percentage at shortstop, second best in the National League. *Baseball America* named him the best defensive shortstop in the league. When he was voted in as a starter in the All-Star Game, it marked the first time in major league history that a shortstop had made the All-Star team in his first two seasons in the big leagues.

The next couple of seasons saw Rollins continue to grow at his position. His batting average steadily grew and speed continued to dictate his game. The 2005 season saw him upping his average to .290, smacking 12 home runs and 11 triples, and adding 41 stolen bases. But the mark he left on baseball was an exciting streak in which he hit safely in the final 36 games of the season. The hitting streak ended at 38 after the first two games of 2006, but a second-half surge helped him raise his average to .277, and he set a Phillies record for home runs for a shortstop with 25.

J-Roll clearly lead by example during his MVP season of 2007 in which the Phillies earned a playoff spot for the first time in 14 years. But he also set the stakes as high as they could be set when in the previous January he stated, "The Mets had a chance to win the World Series last year. Last year is over. I think we are the team to beat in the NL East." As could be expected, those comments were not embraced by Philadelphia's National League neighbors 90 miles to the north. But the Phillies used it as a rallying cry, which may have helped them in their quest for the title. And by the time the Mets late-season collapse ended with a drubbing on the final day of their season, Rollins and the Phillies proved to be the team to beat.

Prior to the start of the 2008 campaign, Rollins was prognosticating again, stating that he felt that his team would win 100 games. While the Phillies failed to do that during the regular season, it should be noted that they did manage to win their hundredth game of 2008—in Game 1 of the World Series. ⑰

Shane Victorino

The 2008 Philadelphia Phillies are a team of strong personalities. There are gentle giants like Ryan Howard, gutsy and gritty quiet types like Chase Utley, guys who shine in the media spotlight like Jimmy Rollins, and a player who leaves it all out on the field as well as being the clown prince of the ball club, outfielder Shane Victorino.

The speedy native of Wailuku, Hawaii, may well be the fastest runner on the club. But possibly more than any other Phillies player, Shane Victorino answered questions about his ability to become an everyday big-league player. During his first two seasons with the club he saw plenty of action, particularly in right field, but occasionally center field. But when Aaron Rowand departed for the San Francisco Giants following the 2007 season, some wondered if Victorino could adequately fill Rowand's shoes in center field.

The Flyin' Hawaiian more than answered the bell in 2008 as evidenced by his career-high .293 batting average in 146 games with 14 homers, 58 RBIs, and 36 stolen bases. Victorino's speed was an element of his game that was never really tapped early in his career. He was a track-and-field star in high school, setting a state record for the 100m, 10.80 seconds. But prior to 2007 the most

bases he had stolen in the major leagues was seven in 2003 in a 36-game stint with the San Diego Padres. Even though he hit .287 in his first full year in the major leagues with the Phillies in 2006, he only stole four sacks and was thrown out three times.

Enter Davey Lopes. The former star second baseman for the Los Angeles Dodgers was hired as the Phillies first-base and base-running coach prior to the 2007 season. All Lopes did in his career was swipe 557 bases, including 77 in 1975 and 63 in 1976. One of the players he took under his wing was Victorino, in an attempt to harness his incredible natural speed and instruct him with the proper base-stealing techniques. The result has been larceny as The Flyin' Hawaiian has been on the run ever since. After stealing only four bases in 2006, he stole 37 in 22 fewer games in 2007, being thrown out just four times. The trend continued in 2008 as Victorino added another 36 steals to his resume.

But stealing bases is far from being Shane Victorino's only talent. Acquired from the Los Angeles Dodgers in the Rule 5 draft in December of 2004, he was viewed as a player with tons of potential who may have not been ready for prime-time action in the big leagues. After five largely inconsistent minor league

"A player who leaves it all out on the field, the speedy Victorino is also known as the clown prince of the ball club."

seasons, he began to put it together with Double AA Jacksonville in 2004, hitting .328 in 75 games. But he struggled after moving up to Triple A Las Vegas, hitting only .235 in 55 games. But his first year with the Phillies organization in 2005 turned the tide of his career. He was named the International League's Most Valuable Player for the Scranton-Wilkes Barre Red Barons. He hit a solid .310 with 18 home runs, 70 RBIs, 16 triples, and 17 stolen bases.

A brief 21-game stint with the Phillies saw him hit .294 with a pair of home runs. The combination of power and speed is a truly rare commodity and Victorino continues to exhibit those two strengths time and again. In his first regular action in the major leagues, he played in 153 games in 2006 and batted .287 with six home runs and 46 RBIs. Victorino became the regular right fielder after the Phillies traded Bobby Abreu to the New York Yankees on July 31 of that year.

Another important aspect of Victorino's game is defense. Thanks to his speed, he can catch up to most any ball hit to the outfield. In addition, he possesses a gun of an arm, which helped him record 10 assists in 2007 from right field, while he then threw out seven more runners from center field in 2008.

While he could not match the power numbers of Abreu in right field, Victorino continued to be a force offensively in 2007. To steal 37 bases you have to get on base and he certainly did that with regularity, hitting .281 with 12 homers, 46 RBIs, and 23 doubles. He seemed to mature as a player with every season, while never losing his fun personality to which teammates and fans alike have taken so strongly.

The move to center field in 2008 to replace Rowand saw Victorino's big-league stock leap. He fielded the position flawlessly, added excitement with a number of circus catches, ran the bases with abandon, and improved as an offensive threat. Again, his combination of speed and power allowed him to hit a career-high 14 home runs plus record eight triples and 36 stolen bases.

As the Phillies continue to be a playoff contender, there will always concern about turnover in the lineup, with new players coming in and working to find their place with the team. That's just the way baseball is in this day and age. While the Phillies will always have concerns about some players, it's a safe bet that they have crossed off any questions about Shane Victorino. He has answered them all and become an outstanding major-league outfielder who should be patrolling center field for the Phillies for years to come. In fact, he may very well become a presence in the All-Star Game.

There is little doubt that Shane Victorino, the Flyin' Hawaiian, is the real deal. ◑

Chris Coste

Chris Coste is a unique phenomenon. That he completed his third season in the major leagues in 2008 as a second-string catcher is nothing out of the ordinary, because every big-league team has at least two catchers on its roster. But that he persevered long enough to be a major leaguer at age 35 is an enormous testament to his character as well as his ability.

Coste split time with Carlos Ruiz behind the plate for most of the 2008 season, hitting .263 in 98 games with nine home runs and 36 RBIs, both career highs. Coste is a dependable player who has become a fine catcher with the ability to be an offensive force either off the bench or in the starting lineup. In fact, when he came into the Phillies' game against the Mets on August 26 in the eighth inning, he went four for four at the plate in the extra-inning affair. Thus he became the first player in 63 years to enter a game that late and garner four hits. He also has a sense for the dramatic—the final of his four hits won the game in the 13th inning for the Phillies.

The Chris Coste story goes much deeper than a treatment of his statistics. The Phillies late, great player and announcer, Hall of Famer Richie Ashburn, used to refer to catching equipment as the tools of ignorance. Starting out his career as a catcher, Ashburn would often relate how difficult being a backstop can be. But Coste is a player who honed his skills behind the plate to give himself a better shot at making it to The Show. But it was a long, interesting journey.

A native of Fargo, North Dakota, Coste was an All-American baseball player at Concordia College in Minnesota. When his collegiate career ended, his long professional pilgrimage began. His resume includes stops in towns such as Brandon, Fargo, Akron, Buffalo, Pawtucket, Indianapolis, Scranton-Wilkes Barre, Clearwater, Reading, Ottawa, and finally Philadelphia. Prior to his Phillies career, Coste was also with the Pirates, Indians, Red Sox, and Brewers organizations. Talk about a jack-of-all-trades: he has caught, played second base, third base, first base, and the outfield, and even pitched five times.

While playing for Fargo for four years, the lowest Coste hit was .312 in 1997 and the best of a number of good seasons came in 1999 when he hit the ball at a .335 clip with 16 home runs and 60 RBIs in 85 games. He was then signed to a contract by the Cleveland Indians organization. His best season there was with Buffalo in 2002 when he hit .318 in 124 games with eight dingers and 67 RBIs. After a year in

"A native of Fargo, North Dakota, Coste was an All-American baseball player at Concordia College in Minnesota."

the Red Sox organization, Coste was with Milwaukee's Indianapolis Triple A farm club and hit .294 in 78 games.

He signed on with the Phillies top minor league club in Scranton-Wilkes Barre in 2005 and responded with an outstanding season, hitting .292 and recording career highs in home runs (20) and RBIs (89). Coste then raised a number of eyebrows thanks to a torrid spring training with the big club in 2006, hitting .463. One of the last players cut from the Phillies at the end of spring training, he returned to Scranton-Wilkes Barre and hoped for the phone to ring, which it finally did. His 12-year journey had finally taken him to the major leagues.

Nothing has ever been easy for Chris Coste and his first big league hit was no different. He finally broke a 0-for-13 slump to get his first hit against James Shields of Tampa Bay. On July 19 he smacked his first home run against San Francisco's Mike Thompson, making him the third non-pitcher in big league history to hit his first homer at age 33 or older, joining Alan Zinter and So Taguchi.

Coste finished his rookie year in the bigs with a .328 average, with seven homers and 32 RBIs. But after his coming out party in 2006, Coste found himself back in the minors at the start of the 2007 season. He spent time in Ottawa, Reading, and Clearwater before coming back to the Phillies for good in June. He responded with a .279 average with five home runs and 22 RBIs, helping the Phillies earn a post-season berth.

Going into spring training in 2008, Coste was assured of his spot on the big league roster, backing up Ruiz. That being said, he was probably relieved when he broke camp with the team. After hitting well for most of the season and sharing time with Ruiz behind the plate, he went into a batting slump for the first time in his major-league career. But he still hit a very respectable .263 with career highs in games (98), at bats (274), hits (72), home runs (9), and RBIs (36). He also added a single in the National League Championship Series against the Los Angeles Dodgers.

After years of tying to prove that he had the right stuff shuffling from one minor league town to the next, Chris Coste has proven that he is a capable big-league catcher and hitter. He has become a cult favorite among fans in Philadelphia, who have embraced him and call themselves the Coste Guard.

There are certainly no tools of ignorance as far as this journeyman ball player is concerned. He wrote his first book, *Hey...I'm Just the Catcher*, in 1997 dealing with his first few seasons playing Independent League baseball and a second book, *The 33-Year-Old Rookie*, in 2008, recounting his first year in the majors with the Phillies. He also won the 2006 Dallas Green Special Achievement Award, presented by the Philadelphia chapter of Baseball Writers Association of America, as well as the Media Good Guy Award from the Philadelphia SportsWriters Association.

In a sports world that has been tarnished by the use of illegal steroids and other performance enhancing substances, as well as countless examples of athletes seemingly falling over each other to exhibit bad behavior, Chris Coste is a refreshing change. He's a throwback to a better time when athletes played for the love of the game and respected the game. Considering his long struggle to make it, there is no doubt about how he feels about baseball. It's rewarding to see baseball finally love him back. ⓞ

35

Cole Hamels

Many baseball scouts and field personnel will swear that left-handed pitchers normally mature late. They are often wild early in their careers, on and off the field, and take a little longer to develop that big league savvy. There is no more significant example of this school of thought than the great Hall of Fame southpaw, Sandy Koufax. He was a talented pitcher who needed years to develop into arguably the most dominant pitcher in the history of the game.

It's still way too early in the career of Phillies left-hander Cole Hamels to compare him to Koufax or another overpowering pitcher like Steve Carlton, but there is little doubt that this talented young phenom may have the right stuff to someday be positioned right next to those two members of baseball's hallowed hall in Cooperstown, New York. Frankly, he has accomplished more than either of the other two pitchers at the same stage of their careers.

Hamels had spent the better part of three years in The Show at the conclusion of the 2008 season, compiling an impressive 38-23 record and an ERA of 3.43. At a similar point in his career, the great Koufax was just 9-10 with a higher ERA, while Steve Carlton, better known in Philadelphia as "Lefty," had a 30-23

mark with an ERA that was better than either Koufax or Hamels. Again, it is much too soon to put Hamels in this class of pitcher, but if he stays healthy there is no telling what he might accomplish.

But if there is one worry about the strapping 6-foot-3, 175-pound Hamels, it is his health. He has already missed parts of two minor league and two major league seasons due to injuries. While that has been a concern for the Phillies organization, Hamels did just complete his busiest season ever with 227 innings pitched without a single physical hitch.

As a junior at Rancho Bernardo High School in San Diego, Hamels' fast ball often topped 94 mps, but when he broke his pitching arm that year, some scouts lost interest in this talented young prospect. Not the Phillies, who drafted him in the first round of the Amateur Draft.

To say that he broke into professional baseball in 2003 with a bang is a gross understatement. Named the recipient of the Paul Owens Award as the best pitcher in the Phillies minor league system, Hamels began his career at Lakewood, going 6-1 with an ERA of .084. In nine of his 13 starts, he did not give up a run, averaging 13.9 strikeouts per every nine innings pitched.

Prior to the start of the 2004 season, Hamels

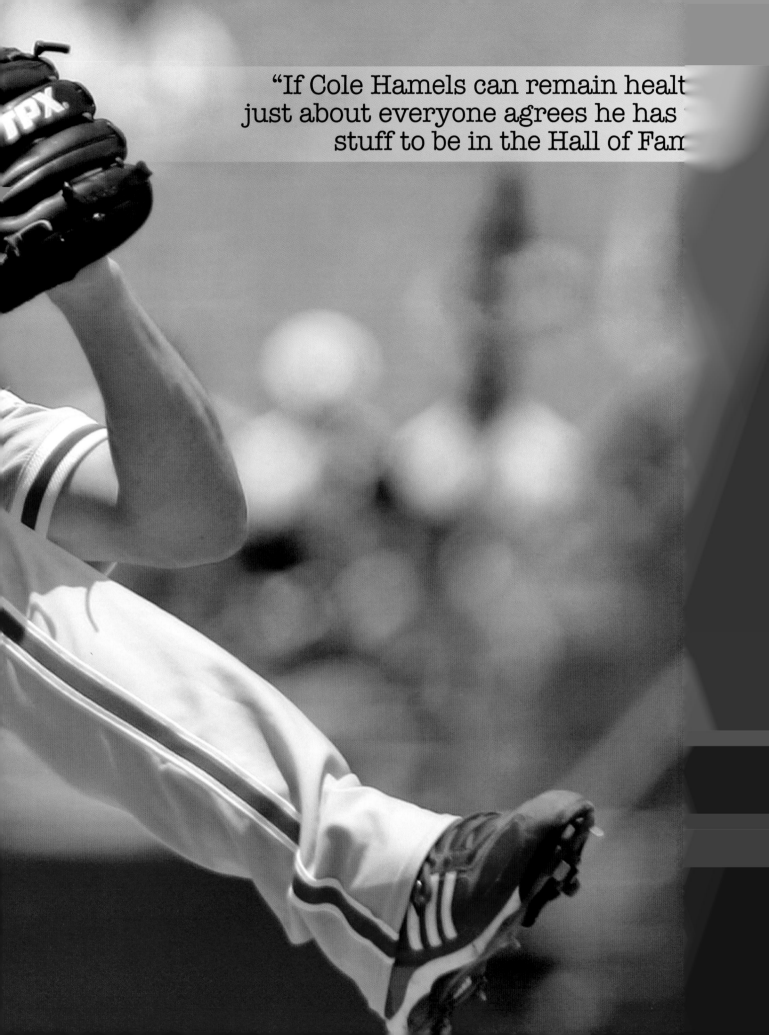

"If Cole Hamels can remain healt
just about everyone agrees he has
stuff to be in the Hall of Fam

was a non-roster invitee to the Phillies major league camp. On March 5 he threw two shutout innings against the powerful New York Yankees. But what garnered much attention was that in his second inning of pitching he struck out Derek Jeter, Alex Rodreguez, and Tony Clark.

Once the season began he was 1-0 with a 1.13 ERA for Clearwater after four games, but the organization shut their top pitching prospect down for the rest of the year due to his second bout with elbow tendonitis.

That he was young and left-handed came into play in 2005. Hamels broke his pitching hand in an altercation in a bar and missed time at the start of the season. When pitching, he was still a top prospect. In six games split between Clearwater and Double A Reading, Hamels was 4-0 with a low ERA. In fact, he finally gave up the first home run of his professional career after his 25th start and 133 innings of homer-less ball. But just as he began to ascend the ladder to the major leagues, a back injury forced him to be shut down for the remainder of the season after a start on July 19 against Portland.

After a couple of disappointing seasons that still showed his incredible potential, the 2006 campaign saw him stay healthy enough, long enough to make it to the major leagues. After a pair of injury-shortened seasons, the Phillies started Hamels at Clearwater where he was 1-1 with a 1.77 ERA before being promoted to Triple A Scranton-Wilkes Barre. Cole Hamels had breezed through every level of the minor leagues. Perhaps Triple A hitters would have their way with him.

That was not to be the case as he went 2-0 with a 0.39 ERA before being called to the major leagues by the Phillies. His minor league career ended with a 14-4 record in 36 games. He threw 201 innings and surrendered just 117 hits and three home runs, walked 74, and struck out 276. By all accounts, Mr. Hamels was ready for The Show.

Upon his recall to the major leagues, Hamels went 9-8 in his rookie season with a 4.08 ERA. He surrendered just 117 hits in 132 innings with 145 strikeouts, but Hamels was not used to such rough treatment.

He "rebounded" in his sophomore year with a glittering 15-5 mark and a 3.39 ERA, cementing his position as the ace of the Phillies staff. He helped guide the team to the post-season and although he lost his lone play-off start against the Rockies, he pitched well.

The 2008 year got off to a troubling start for the stylish left-hander with a 94 mph fastball and an All-Star caliber change-up when he expressed his unhappiness with his contract situation, calling the Phillies contract a low blow. In spite of his contract situation, Cole Hamels blossomed into one of the best pitchers in the game. He was the ace of the Phillies staff with a 14-10 record with two shutouts and a 3.09 ERA. In a career high 227 innings, he yielded just 193 hits and 53 walks while fanning 196. But he suffered from a severe case of lack of offensive support from his teammates. That 14-10 record could have easily been 18-6.

Judging by his professional approach, improved health, and absolutely phenomenal season and post-season, there is little doubt that Cole Hamels has become one of the elite pitchers in the game. Perhaps Mr. Koufax and Mr. Carlton should take notice. ⓞ

Brett Myers

The Phillies' rise to the top of the National League's Eastern Division has been fueled by a strong contingent of home-grown players. This core group includes Pat Burrell, Ryan Howard, Jimmy Rollins, Carlos Ruiz, Chase Utley, Cole Hamels, J.A. Happ, Kyle Kendrick, Ryan Madson, and big, right-handed pitcher Brett Myers. Every team needs the right mix of ingredients to be successful, but raising and nurturing products of your own farm system is a sure-fire way to survive and succeed in baseball today. And as much as any member of the 2008 Phillies, Brett Myers epitomizes the ideas of surviving and succeeding.

Myers' 2008 season has taken him on a roller-coaster ride. After finishing 2007 as the club's closer out of the bullpen, Myers returned to the starting rotation in a move that proved more difficult than anyone hoped. His 2008 season included being the Phillies starter on Opening Day, a month-long winless streak that culminated with a stint in the minor leagues, a return to the majors with a great string of games, a playoff win, and a World Series berth. But Myers seems to have come through it all unscathed and a bit wiser for the experience. Considering where he was earlier in the year, his 10–13 mark in 2008 is a pretty impressive accomplishment.

Myers was selected by the Phillies in the first round (12th overall) of the amateur draft in June 1999. After seven games with the Phillies Gulf Coast League team that summer, he spent the 2000 season with Piedmont, in the South Atlantic League. He went 13–7 with a 3.18 ERA in 27 games, fanning 140 batters in 175 innings.

That stellar performance earned him a promotion to the Phillies' Double A club in Reading in 2001. Myers proved to be more than up for the challenge as evidence by his 13–4 record with 130 strikeouts in 156 innings. He began the 2002 season at Triple A Scranton-Wilkes Barre posting a 9–6 record with an ERA of 3.59 in 19 games. At that point, the organization decided he was ready for The Show. The organization was right.

Myers made his big-league debut on May 24, 2002, at Wrigley Field in Chicago. Eight innings later Brett Myers left the game having surrendered just two hits and one run, earning his first win, 4–1. He started 11 more games that season and finished the year with a 4–5 mark and a respectable 4.25 ERA.

In 2003, his first full season in the major leagues, Myers won a career-high 14 games against 9 losses with a 4.43 ERA. In 32 starts he threw 193 innings and fanned 143 hitters. At

"Myers roller-coaster season saw him return to the starting rotation, get sent to the minors, and ultimately emerge as a gritty presence late in the season."

the ripe old age of 22, he was also the youngest pitcher to open the season in the Phillies starting rotation since Calvin Maduro in 1997.

The 2004 season saw Myers complete the year with an 11-11 record and a high ERA of 5.52. But he suffered from a lack of offensive support from his teammates, which culminated in a five-start losing streak in which he had a total of 14 Phillies' runs to work with.

Still a young pitcher of 24, Myers rebounded nicely in 2005 with a 13-8 record and a fine 3.72 ERA. Using his hard fast ball and devastating curve, he struck out 208 batters in 215 innings. His development continued as he set new career highs not only for strikeouts, but starts (34), innings, complete games (2) and ERA. And he was the first Phillies pitcher since Curt Schilling in 1998 to eclipse the 200 strikeout mark. He was also a pitcher who was able to help himself at the plate, recording 11 sacrifices and 10 hits.

A year older in 2006, Myers learned that life is a learning experience. It's not making mistakes that should mark us, but how we react to them. For the fourth consecutive season, he won in double digits with a 12-7 record and an ERA of 3.91. Continuing his development as a strikeout pitcher, he fanned 189 in 198 innings. He won five consecutive road starts in the second half of the season. But controversy followed Myers after an incident that occurred on June 23 of that year in Boston. He was placed on the inactive list for two weeks in order to tend to a personal situation. By all accounts, he reacted in the best form possible.

One of the fondest memories that this generation of Phillies fans have is Brett Myers striking out Willie Mo Pena of the Washington Nationals for the final out to preserve a 6-1 victory and put the Phillies into the playoffs in 2007. Myers was finishing out the game because the team's original closer in 2007, Tom Gordon, had been on the disabled list for nearly three months, forcing the Phillies to adjust their pitching staff. Myers was named the closer on May 2. He loved the challenge and was lights out. He compiled a 5-7 record that year with 21 saves. When Gordon returned to the active roster, he became the set-up man for Myers. They were an effective tandem that helped the team get into the playoffs.

Myers loved closing and was prepared for that to be his new spot until the Phillies acquired premier closer Brad Lidge in a trade from Houston. Any thoughts of Myers holding on to the closer's role immediately disappeared. He was returning to the starting rotation. Given the honor of starting on Opening Day, things did not work out as planned for Myers and he struggled with the change in roles. He finally agreed to go to the minor leagues for a short stay to attempt to work on his mechanics away from the major-league pressure cooker. Once again, Myers reacted like a pro, returning to the Phillies and going on a 7-2 run with a 1.80 ERA—a performance that ultimately led his team to the playoffs and the World Series. ⚾

50

Jamie Moyer

Jamie Moyer has proven that apparently you can go home again. A native of Sellersville, Pennsylvania, not far from Philadelphia, Moyer left the area to pursue his professional baseball career in 1984. He had enjoyed a stellar career at Philadelphia's St. Joseph's University, where his number 10 was retired by the Hawks baseball program. It took 22 years to come home, but in 2006 Moyer saw one of his childhood dreams realized when the Seattle Mariners sent the veteran southpaw to the Phillies in exchange for pitchers Andrew Baldwin and Andrew Barb.

Between St. Joe's and his trade back home, Moyers made major-league stops in Chicago, Texas, St. Louis, Baltimore, Boston, and Seattle. And while he won 211 games prior to the trade to Philadelphia, it's doubtful that anyone expected him to have increased that total by 35 by the end of the 2008 season. In addition, it's seriously doubtful if General Manager Pat Gillick expected Moyer to lead the staff in wins this year with a 16-7 record and a 3.71 ERA. Not too shabby for a 45-year-old.

In 2008, Moyer became the second-oldest player to pitch for the Phillies; the oldest was 47-year-old Kaiser Wilhelm, who came out of retirement to pitch four games in 1921. He became the oldest pitcher to earn a win for the Phillies

when he won his debut with the team, nudging Jerry Koosman out of the eldest-winning-pitcher spot. But with age comes experience. Though this savvy southpaw rarely hits 80 mph on his fastball, his collection of off-speed pitches and breaking stuff often has opposing hitters overanxious and helping him out by swinging at balls they have little chance of hitting well. While he is 35-21 in his two-plus years with the Phillies, his 246-185 career mark shows what this 22-year veteran is all about.

It took Jamie Moyer five years to make it to the major leagues, which he did in 1986 with the Chicago Cubs, recording a 7-4 record that season. He followed that up with a 12-15 record in 1987, his first full big-league season. Following a 9-15 mark in 1988 when he had an excellent ERA of 3.48, Moyers was involved in a major trade. He was dealt along with outfielder Rafael Palmeiro and pitcher Drew Hall to Texas in exchange for infielders Curtis Wilkerson and Luis Benitez, pitchers Mitch Williams and Paul Kilgus, and outfielder Pablo Delgado.

The change in scenery was not a good one for Moyer. He spent three months on the disabled list in 1989, winning only four games. Finally after two frustrating seasons in Texas with a combined record of 6 wins and 15 losses, he was released and signed by the St.

The ageless, tireless Moyer went 16-7 in 2008 and pitched 196.1 innings—the second most on the team.

Louis Cardinals. An equally disappointing 1991 saw him record a 0-5 record in St. Louis and a 5-10 mark with the Cardinals' Louisville farm club. Free agency was followed by stints with the Cubs and Tigers organizations that could have easily seen a lesser man call it quits. But Moyer eventually signed a free-agent contract with the Baltimore Orioles that help resurrect his career.

After starting the 1993 season in the minor leagues, Moyer was recalled to the Orioles and went 12-9 with a 3.43 ERA. The next two seasons saw him with a 13-13 combined record and he stayed with Baltimore through the 1995 season, when the Red Sox signed him to a contract. The lefty was 7-1 with Boston, which led the Mariners to deal outfielder Darren Bragg even up for the veteran hurler. Moyer then went 6-2 for Seattle, starting an 11-year stretch in the Pacific Northwest which saw Moyer win 145 games.

His stay in Seattle included a 17-5 season in 1997, 20-6 in 2001 at age 38, 21-7 two years later, and 13-7 in 2005. When he got off to a 6-12 start with the Mariners in 2006, Seattle was finally willing to trade their Ancient Mariner to his hometown team. In eight games with the Phillies that year, Moyer went 5-2 with a 4.03 ERA—good enough for Philadelphia to sign him to a two-year contract extension.

Anxious to extend his career now that he was back in the National League, Moyer went 14-12 in 2007, helping the Phillies in their playoff drive. In fact, facing Washington on the final day of the season with the team desperately needing a win, the Phillies pinned their playoff hopes on the shoulder of this crafty lefty. The New York Mets, also fighting for a playoff spot, turned to their own veteran pitcher, Tom Glavine. Unfortunately for the Mets, Glavine never got out of the first inning against the Florida Marlins and their playoff hopes were dashed. Meanwhile, Phillies old-timer Moyer won his game, and he also contributed six strong innings in the NLDS against Colorado.

No matter what a pitcher accomplished the previous season, when he is 45 years old—as Moyer was at the start of the 2008 season—there are serious concerns about his ability to perform at a high level. It's safe to say that Jamie Moyer did not pitch at the 2007 level in 2008—in fact, he took it a step higher, as his 16 wins against only seven losses indicates. He barely missed pitching 200 innings, falling just four short. Not bad for a guy who was the oldest active player in major league baseball. And when he singled off San Diego's Chris Young on April 30, he became the oldest Phillies' player to ever get a hit.

While time certainly waits for no man, it's also very true that Jamie Moyer has gotten better with age. And now, 24 years after he began his professional odyssey, he has come home the owner of 246 career wins and a start in his second World Series—a solid Game 3 no-decision performance in a hard-fought Phillies' victory. ⚾

54

Brad Lidge

Coming off their first playoff appearance in 14 years in 2007, the Phillies had seemingly found a new closer: Brett Myers. When veteran Tom Gordon went on the disabled list early in the season, Myers—immensely talented but struggling as a starter—was tabbed as the new closer. All he did was accept the role and convert 21 saves. But the Philadelphia organization had its eyes on a closing prize that had become available in Houston, Brad "Lights Out" Lidge.

In November 2007, the Phillies acquired Lidge from Houston along with infielder/outfielder Eric Bruntlett in exchange for pitcher Geoff Geary, speedy outfielder Michael Bourn, and infield prospect Mike Costanzo. Myers was pushed back into the starting rotation, Tom Gordon remained the set-up man (which he'd become after returning from injury), and Brad Lidge became the Phillies ninth-inning man.

In life and especially in closing baseball games, it's often a case of, "What have you done for us lately?" While Lidge had accumulated 123 saves in five years with Houston, he was demoted from the closer's role for a time with the Astros in 2007 and while he did save 19 games, he blew eight other save opportunities. That performance opened the door for the trade to the Phillies. And though he arrived in Philadelphia with a surgically repaired knee that needed more minor surgery in spring training, he also arrived in town with his closer's "light's out" attitude in-tact.

Lidge was dominant the entire 2008 season with a 2-0 record and an ERA of 1.95. He silenced all his doubters in Houston by converting 41 saves out of 41 save opportunities during his first season with the Phillies. In other words, he was perfect. His overpowering fastball and knee-buckling slider made most hitters appear thoroughly overmatched all season long. Lidge pitched in 72 games and struck out 92 hitters in 69 innings. He also gave up just 50 hits and yielded only two home runs. At the end of the season he was awarded the National League's Comeback Player of the Year Award.

Lidge's transformation was evident from the start, so much so that the Phillies organization avoided any chance of losing him to free agency by signing him to a three-year $37.5 million contract extension on June 6. The sudden added wealth and peace of mind over his immediate future did nothing to lessen the killer instinct that he displayed on the pitcher's mound.

Lidge was selected by the Houston Astros as their first-round pick (17th overall) in the 1998 amateur draft. Injuries such as a torn

A lot was at stake when the Phillies signed him in the offseason, but Lidge punched through the pressure with 41 saves and a 1.95 ERA.

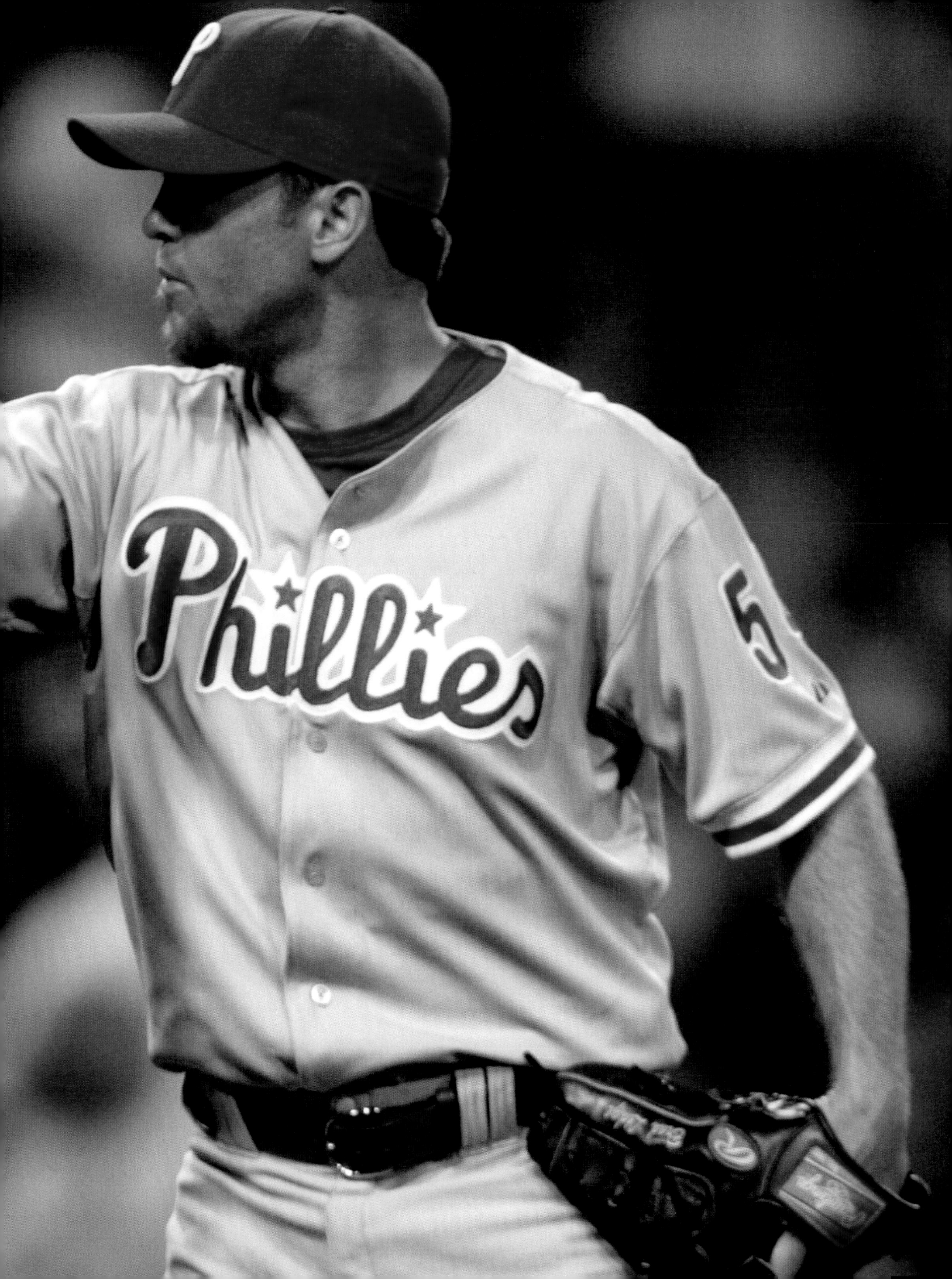
Phillies

rotator cuff and a broken arm limited him to just 23 appearances in his first four professional seasons. But when he was able to pitch, he was very effective, never having an ERA over 3.38.

A healthy Lidge pitched well for three different teams in 2002. He was a combined 6-6 in 29 games for Round Rock of the Texas League and Triple A New Orleans of the Pacific Coast League. He made his major-league debut with the Astros that same year and posted a 1-0 record in six games.

He was healthy and in the major leagues to stay in 2003, sporting a 6-3 record with a 3.60 ERA in 78 appearances for Houston. He was voted the Astros Rookie of the Year by the Houston Chapter of the Baseball Writers Association of America. He also was the winning pitcher in a no-hitter that saw six Astros pitchers shut down the New York Yankees. Lidge combined with Roy Oswalt, Pete Munro, Kirk Saarloos, Octavio Dotel, and Billy Wagner in the gem. He also nailed down his first save.

Lidge became the club's closer in 2004 going 6-5 with a stingy 1.90 ERA with 29 saves in 80 games. His explosive stuff was also evident as he struck out 157 hitters in 94 innings, breaking the National League record for strikeouts for a reliever (151) set by Goose Gossage in 1977. He was also 1-0 in seven playoff games with three saves.

Lidge continued to progress and impress in 2005 with another impressive season. He went 4-4 with a 2.29 ERA and his career high 42 saves in 70 games. He also struck out 103 hitters in 70.2 innings. Lidge joined Wagner as the only Astros' pitchers to save at least 40 games in a season. The Astros reached the playoffs again and while Lidge pitched well in the NLDS, he struggled in the NLCS and World Series.

In the fifth game of the NLCS against the St. Louis Cardinals, Albert Pujols tagged Lidge for a majestic three-run blast to force a sixth game in St. Louis, which Houston won to advance to their World Series. In the Fall Classic, the Astros ran into a hot Chicago White Sox team that swept them in four consecutive games. In the second game of the World Series, Lidge gave up a walk-off game-winning home run to Scott Posednik.

Amid concerns of how the two post-season dingers would affect him, Lidge went 1-5 with an unusually high ERA of 5.28 in 2006. In spite of that, he still amassed 32 saves, blowing six.

While Lidge rebounded somewhat with a 5-3 record during his final year in Houston in 2007, the blown saves became an issue and it was apparent that he would benefit from a change of scenery. After his first fantastic season in Philadelphia, it seems that he likes the scenery in Philadelphia just fine.

Lidge was the only closer in club history to be perfect without blowing a single save all season. Lidge was also the first major-league closer since Eric Gagne to have a perfect conversion rate with at least 30 saves. The next time anyone asks what Brad Lidge has done lately, the answer is a perfect season—which for the Phillies, means a trip to the World Series. ⊙

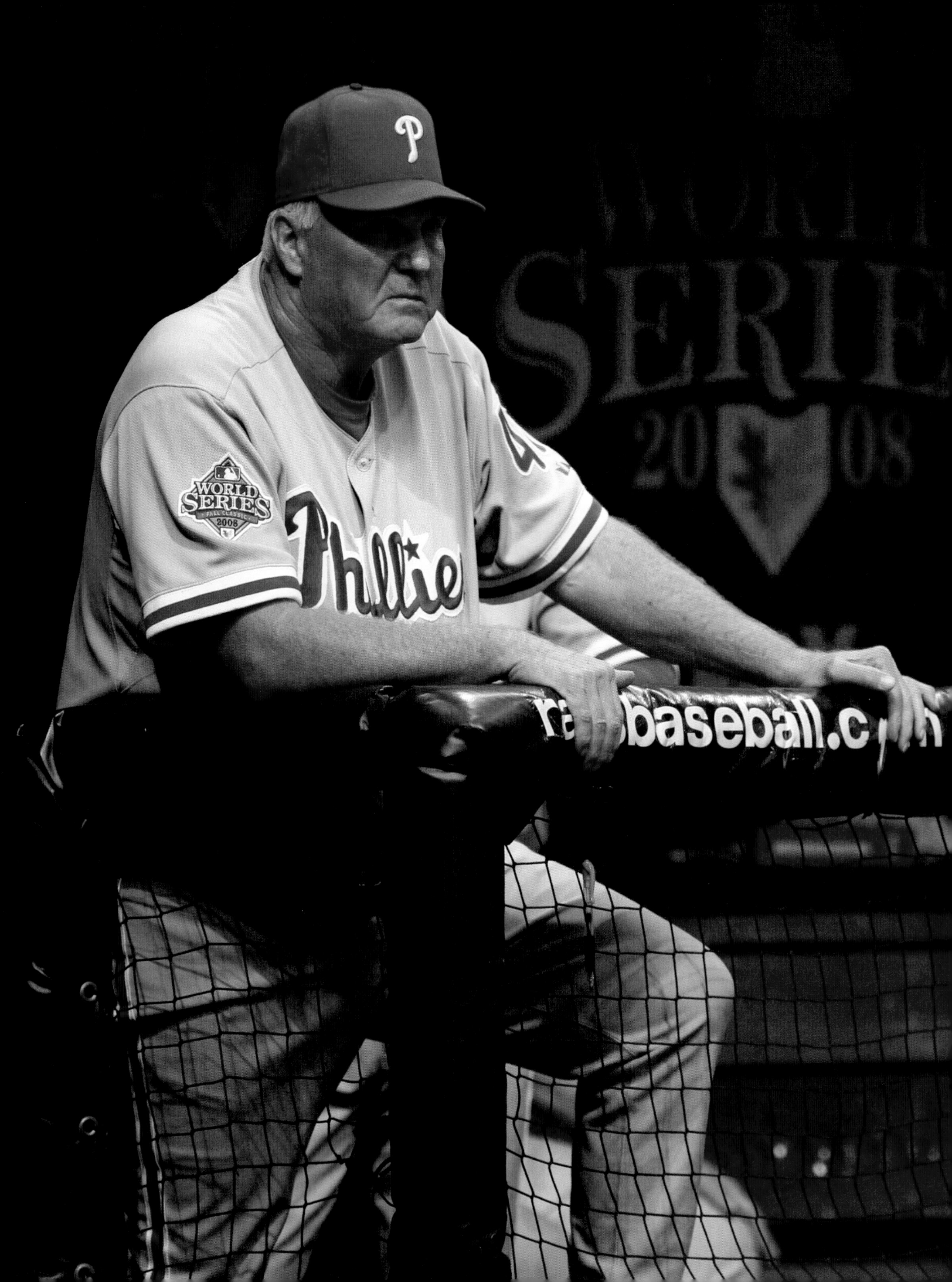
P
WORLD SERIES
FALL CLASSIC
2008
Phillies
SERIE
20 08

Charlie Manuel

Charlie Manual is the kind of guy you'd like to living in the house next door. He's funny, humble, and a genuinely good person. Of course, if you happen to be a fan of the Philadelphia Phillies, he'd also be a great source for playoff and World Series tickets.

A baseball lifer who has an uncanny ability to get players to give their all for him, Charlie Manuel is easy to underestimate. He's a big guy with a strong Southern drawl, courtesy of his roots in Northfork, West Virginia. But to underestimate him is a mistake, as his 574–485 major league managerial record indicates. Much like general manager Pat Gillick, Manuel wins everywhere he goes. In seven seasons as a big-league skipper, his teams have finished in first place three times, second place three times, and third place once. Those results speak for themselves. Charlie Manuel is a winner.

Entering his third year at the helm of the Phillies in 2008, Manuel hoped to get his team over the hump. His team barely missed out on the playoffs in 2006, just three games out of the wild card. After a bad start in 2007, the Phillies got hot in September and overtook a Mets team that folded in an epic collapse to win the National League East Division—only to be swept by the white-hot Colorado Rockies

in the NLDS. But the three-game playoff experience against Colorado had given his club a taste of the good life.

Manuel saw his 2008 Phillies lead the division for much of the season. But after the Mets fired manager Willie Randolph, probably as much for their 2007 collapse as for their disappointing start in 2008, new skipper Jerry Manuel (no relation to Charlie) rallied his troops into a first-place run that had the Phillies looking up in the standings at their neighbors to the north. But once again the Mets saw a late-season lead disappear and Charlie Manuel's squad won the East Division with a 92–70 record.

After their humbling experience against the Rockies in the 2007 playoffs, the Phillies locker room was subdued after clinching the post-season in 2008. Yes, they had defended their NL East title by winning the division, but there was work to be done.

In the NLDS they easily rolled past a good Milwaukee Brewers team. Then they defeated the Los Angeles Dodgers in the NLCS to earn a berth in the Fall Classic. And all the time, Charlie Manuel remained Charlie Manuel. And if his team and the city had not gained enough respect and affection for the Skip, millions of hearts went out to him when his beloved

mother, June, passed away on October 10 at the age of 87. Manuel didn't miss a game, but buried his mother in between playoff series.

Charlie Manuel grew up in West Virginia and was a two-sport star in high school. While he had the talent and the grades to attend the University of Pennsylvania, he spurned offers from the Pittsburgh Pirates, Detroit Tigers, and New York Yankees to sign a free-agent contract with the Minnesota Twins in 1963. He was a good enough student-athlete that in 1995 he was inducted into the Salem-Roanoke Baseball Hall of Fame.

Manuel made his way up through the Twins' minor-league system with mixed results until 1967 and 1968 when he smacked 15 and 13 homers respectively for Wisconsin Rapids and Charlotte. That earned him a spot on the 1969 Twins team that also reached the playoffs. Manuel's rookie season was not a great one: he hit .207 with two home runs and 24 RBIs in 83 games. He was up and down with the Twins and their minor-league affiliates over the next three years before playing briefly for the Los Angeles Dodgers in 1974 and 1975.

That's when Charlie Manuel made one of the best decisions relating to his playing career when he signed with the Yakult Swallows in Japan. In his six seasons in Japan with Yakult and the Kinetsu Buffaloes, he hit .303 with 189 home runs and 491 RBIs. His two greatest seasons began in 1979 when he boasted a .324 average with a league-leading 37 home runs and 94 RBIs, becoming the first American player to be named the Pacific League MVP. The following season, his smacked the ball at a .325 clip and led the league in home runs (48) and RBIs (129).

Upon his return to the United States, Manuel (affectionately known as The Red Devil in Japan because of his hard style of play) began a nine-year managing career in the minor leagues in towns such as Wisconsin Rapids, Orlando, Toledo, Portland, Colorado Springs, and Charlotte. He also spent two-plus seasons managing the Cleveland Indians, who reached the World Series under his tenure.

He joined the Phillies as a special assistant to the general manager and was named the club's 51st manager prior to the 2005 season after Larry Bowa was let go. That season Manuel guided the team to second-place finish with an 88-74 record. That was the highest victory total by a first year Phillies manager since Pat Corrales saw his 1982 team win 89 games.

Manuel's 2006 club won three fewer games and also finished in second place. While there was continued frustration over the club's ability to get over that playoff hump, there were some who noted that Manuel's 173-151 record in his first two seasons as Phillies manager was the most of any team skipper in his first two years since Pat Moran had 181 wins in 1915-1916. Finally, the frustration ended in 2007 as the Phillies reached the playoffs for the first time in 14 years. And the 2008 squad went above and beyond by becoming the first Phillies team to reach the World Series since 1993.

Through it all Charlie Manuel has remained true to himself and endeared himself to the people of Philadelphia—no small feat in a city whose fans once booed Santa Claus! ◯

Pat Gillick

General managers have the toughest job in baseball, though many fans probably don't appreciate their efforts. They answer not just for wins and losses, but also by the job the manager does and also by the contributions made by players they acquired. Judging the performance of individual players seems pretty simple. It should be easy to determine a player's worth by looking at the things that show up in the box score, such as batting average and RBIs for hitters and wins, saves, or even quality starts for pitchers. But general managers also have to look for those things that don't show up in the box score, things that help teams win ballgames: for example, moving runners into scoring position by hitting the ball to the right side of the infield, or distracting the opposing pitcher and catcher as a base-runner.

It appears that Pat Gillick, has aced the test of being Phillies general manager. He has enjoyed remarkable success in his three years on the job. The Phillies, long considered an underachieving franchise (especially in a major baseball market), have won consecutive National League East Division titles and advanced to the World Series in 2008. One of his first and best decisions was to keep Charlie Manuel as manager, and the players he has acquired have almost always made the team better.

This kind of success is nothing new to Pat Gillick. Wherever he's been involved with a team, they've made it into the post-season. He brings winners to town. It's an amazing streak of success.

In 1976 Gillick was scouting director for the New York Yankees. They won the pennant. In his 18 years with the Toronto Blue Jays, the team reached the playoffs five times, winning the World Series in 1992 and 1993 (in the latter year, sadly, over the Phillies). He spent three years in Baltimore and the Orioles made the post-season twice. Gillick then moved on to Seattle where the Mariners made the playoffs twice. And now he has led the Phillies to two playoff appearances in three years. It's a success potion that some wish he could bottle and sell to other major-league organizations.

That's not to say that all of Gillick's moves have worked out. There are those who point to the acquisitions of Freddy Garcia and Adam Eaton, a pair of pitchers who failed to pitch to their potential after being brought to Philadelphia. But failures like those are dwarfed by Gillick's successes. Take a look at the Phillies' World Series roster and you will see Gillick's fingerprints all over it. He traded for Joe Blanton, Eric Bruntlett, Scott Eyre, Brad Lidge, Jamie Moyer, and Matt Stairs. He

signed free agents Chad Durbin, Pedro Feliz, Geoff Jenkins, J.C. Romero, Rudy Seanez, So Taguchi, and Jayson Werth. Last but certainly not least, he claimed a guy who has become the best pinch-hitter in the league, Greg Dobbs, off waivers from Seattle.

Gillick has been in professional baseball for 51 years. A left-handed pitcher for the University of Southern California, he was a member of the NCAA College World Series championship team in 1958. That same year he joined the Orioles minor-league system under Earl Weaver. Gillick went as far as Triple A accumulating a 45-32 record with a 3.42 ERA.

Gillick started his front office career in 1963 as the assistant farm director with the Houston Colt 45's. He spent a decade working for the Astros before accepting the position of coordinator of player development and scouting director with the Yankees in 1974. Gillick stayed in the position until August 1976 when he was named vice president of player personnel for the expansion Toronto Blue Jays. He became the team's first GM at the age of 38.

His teams showed remarkable success, which followed him from Toronto to Baltimore, Seattle, and finally to Philadelphia. Those close to the game have always understood and appreciated Gillick's talent for building winners. The awards and tributes keep flowing in as well. In 2001, Baseball America named him Executive of the Past 20 Years. The following January, he received the Executive Lifetime Achievement Award from the Professional Baseball Scouts Foundation and later that year was added to the Toronto Blue Jays Level of Excellence, the organization's most prestigious award. And following his first season as GM of the Phillies, he was honored once again by Baseball America as one of the 25 most influential people in baseball from 1981-2006.

To put Gillick's accomplishments in a different form, the cumulative record for all of the teams for which he has served as general manager is a remarkable 2,276 wins and 1,993 losses.

The reason for such success comes from experience and judgment. One of the first moves that he made as GM of the Phillies involved a decision at first base. Gentleman Jim Thome, a popular and talented first baseman, had been signed to a huge free-agent contract. But after two very productive years in Philadelphia, he missed significant time due to an elbow injury that opened the door for Ryan Howard to play every day and earn Rookie of the Year honors. Do you keep the veteran? Trade the already-accomplished rookie?

Gillick decided to go with youth by dealing Thome and a fist-full of dollars to the Chicago White Sox for Aaron Rowand and pitching prospects Gio Gonzalez and Daniel Haigwood. In the finest tradition of the game of baseball, the trade has worked out extremely well for both clubs.

The most controversial part of Pat Gillick's three year tenure as GM of the Phillies might well be his announcement earlier during the 2008 season that he intended to step down and retire at the conclusion of the year. In spite of the presence in the Phillies' organization of a number of highly qualified candidates to replace him—including Ruben Amaro Jr. and Mike Arbuckle—it seems prudent for management to try to talk Gillick into staying on board for another year or two.

If that happens, it is not out of the question that Gillick's Philadelphia Phillies might one day be considered a baseball dynasty. ⊘

Season Review

Officially, the Philadelphia Phillies were scheduled to open their 2008 baseball season on March 31 against the Washington Nationals. But their journey to successfully defend the National League East Division title they had won in 2007 started a couple of months prior the regular season. That's when New York Mets outfielder Carlos Beltran threw down the gauntlet and drew a line in the Eastern Division sand.

Beltran stated that even before the Mets acquired Johann Santana they had a chance to win the division crown. But with Santana in the starting rotation there was no doubt the Mets were going to win. He then made it personal by saying directly to Phillies shortstop Jimmy Rollins that the Mets were the team to beat in 2008.

That, of course, was a reference to Rollins' comments prior to the 2007 campaign that the Phillies were the team to beat in the NL East. At least prior to the start of this past season, Rollins had been proven correct.

The Phillies started the season in April by winning at least one game of each series they played, finishing the month 15-12. Always seemingly a slow-starting team, a winning record in the month of April seemed like a good sign to faithful fans in Philadelphia. The good start was even more impressive considering that Rollins and scrappy outfielder Shane Victorino missed time due to injuries. Newly acquired reserve infielder/outfielder Eric Bruntlett proved an able replacement for Rollins, the defending National League Most Valuable Player.

Second baseman Chase Utley hit well over .300 with 11 home runs in April and left fielder Pat Burrell also got off to a strong start. And the pitching staff, anchored by ace left-hander Cole Hamels, performed well. The new kid on the block in the bullpen, former Houston closer Brad Lidge, was perfect.

May was an even better month for the Phillies as their 18-13 record indicated. The offense started to get in gear as Ryan Howard slugged 10 home runs and Jayson Werth began to make a case for playing every day—before being injured and spending time on the disabled list. They ended the month with an offense explosion knocking off the Astros in Houston 15-6, before returning home to clobber Colorado 20-5 and elevate Jamie Moyer to a 5-3 record. Just two months into the season, the Phillies were flying high with a 32-25 record.

As good as May was, June threatened to be ever better as the Phillies started out gangbusters. They continued to hit and pitch so well that they reached a record of 41-30 on the 15th of the month. But a not-so-funny thing happened on the way to a great month—Interleague Play. That old Phillies bugaboo continued to haunt them. They lost two-of-three to Boston, three-in-row to the Angels and two-of-three to

....

Charlie Manuel talks with former manager Dallas Green on the first day of the team's baseball spring training for pitchers and catchers in Clearwater, Florida, on February 14, 2008.

Ryan Howard signs autographs before a spring training baseball game against the Pittsburgh Pirates in Bradenton, Florida, in March 2008.

both Oakland and Texas. The promising start of June was forgotten during a 3–9 stretch that dropped the Phillies' monthly tally below .500 for the first time in the season.

What else could be better for a struggling team than the Atlanta Braves? The Phillies feasted on once-mighty Atlanta, sweeping a three-game set to open the month of July—a result that reflected the sweeping change of power that has taken place in the NL East. They got good performances from Cole Hamels, who improved to 9–5 and Kyle Kendrick, who improved to 8–3. Naturally, the Phillies were brought back to Earth by the Mets, who won three of four. But the Phils made a nice comeback prior to the All-Star Game by winning their next two series to post a 52–44 record at the break.

Knowing that you simply can't have enough good starting pitching, general manager Pat Gillick engineered what proved to be an important deal by acquiring the Oakland Athletics Opening Day pitcher, talented young right-hander Joe Blanton, in exchange for three minor league prospects: infielder Adrain Cardenas, outfielder Matt Spencer, and pitcher Josh Outman. The deal was considered to be a step in the right direction for the Phillies, who in Blanton got an experienced pitcher who is still young enough to have a positive impact on the club for a number of years.

Following the All-Star break, which the

(opposite) Fans greet members of the 2008 Philadelphia Phillies as they enter the field before their home opener against the Washington Nationals in Philadelphia on March 31, 2008. (above) The Phillies celebrate with Pat Burrell after he hit a game-winning two-run home run against the San Francisco Giants in the 10th inning on May 2, 2008. The Phillies won 6–5.

Ryan Howard scores the winning run as the throw to San Francisco Giants catcher Steve Holm goes wide in the ninth inning of a game in May 2008. The Phillies won 6-5. Giants' closing pitcher Kelichi Yabu is at left.

American League won to ensure home-field advantage in the World Series, the Phillies lost consecutive series to the Marlins and Mets. The newly acquired Blanton kept the Phillies in the only game in which they won against New York. But they won two of three from the Braves and swept the Nationals to end the month on a positive note and improve their record to 10 games over .500 at 59–49. There was a buzz in the air as things seemed to be looking up. It looked as if the Phillies were primed to have a strong second half to guaran-

tee yet another post-season excursion.

Next in store for the team were the dog days of August. They responded with a 16–13 month that included the kind of highlights and lowlights that are typical in a long season. Joe Blanton got a win against the Cardinals to help the Phils take two-of-three. They did the same against Florida with Kyle Kendrick pitching well and winning. But their West Coast swing was a difficult one as Manny Ramirez and the Dodgers won four straight from the Phillies at Chavez Ravine. But they rebounded nicely to

(above) Chase Utley's maple bat shatters during a game against the Colorado Rockies in May 2008. (opposite) Utley goes airborne to avoid a takeout attempt by the Arizona Diamondbacks' Justin Upton in a May 2008 game in Phoenix.

Chase Utley barrels through the Cincinnati Reds' David Ross while trying to score from first on a double by Ryan Howard in the third inning of a game in late June 2008.

win a series win in San Diego, where Moyer improved his record to 11-7 and Hamels upped his mark to 10-8. They followed the San Diego trip by taking a series from Washington before the Dodgers came to town.

In what appeared to be a possible playoff preview, the Phillies returned the favor to Los Angeles for their sweep out west by winning four straight at home. Hamels and Kendrick both notching their 11th victories, and a resurgent Brett Myers won his seventh game. The team split with the Cubs, with Moyer earning his 12th victory of the year and Myers getting number eight. It was a good August for the Phillies; they ended the month at 75-62.

Taking a page from their previous September, the Phils went 17-8 in the season's final month to roar back and once again capture the East Division crown. They won two-of-three from the Mets as Myers continued to pitch well and up his record to 9-10. Jamie Moyer also won a game, making the ageless wonder 13-7 for the season.

Then the Phillies swept four-straight games from the Brewers, a result that cost Milwaukee manager Ned Yost his job. Moyer won his 14th game of the year, while Hamels got number 13 and Myers number 10. Then they swept the Braves in Atlanta and took a series from Florida, with Blanton and Moyer getting the wins.

As the month wore down, the Phillies made it a little tougher for themselves by losing two out of three games to Atlanta, but once again an epic collapse by the New York Mets made things a lot easier. The Phillies defeated Washington behind Joe Blanton who got his ninth win of the season and Jamie Moyer, who notched his 16th win, and clinched the division> Les Walrond earned his first victory of the season in the finale.

If Carlos Beltran had been correct and the New York Mets were the team to beat in 2008, the Phillies successfully completed the task—and for the second year in a row.

The Phillies finished the season 92-70. Charlie Manuel's four-year record as manager of the Phillies now stood at 354-294. On the pitcher's mound, Jamie Moyer led the staff with a 16-7 record, Cole Hamels was 14-10, Brett Myers 10-13, and Joe Blanton 4-0. J.C. Romero appeared in 81 games and was 4-4 with a 2.75 ERA. Ryan Madson finished at 4-2 in 76 games with a 3.05 ERA. And the closer, Brad Lidge, was 2-0 with a 1.95 ERA in 72 games, but more importantly he posted 41 saves in 41 opportunities and 92 strikeouts in 69.1 innings.

Pinch-hitting specialist Greg Dobbs led the team with a .301 average with 9 homers and 40 RBIs. Shane Victorino hit .293 with 14 home runs and 58 RBI's. Chase Utley hit .292 with 33 home runs and 104 RBIs. Jayson Werth hit .273 with 24 home runs and 67 RBIs. Pat Burrell hit .250 with 33 home runs and 86 RBIs. And Ryan Howard hit .251 with a league leading 48 home runs and a league leading 146 RBIs. Considering how many players made solid contributions during the season, the 2008 NL East title was truly a team effort for the Phillies. ⓞ

Pat Burrell follows through on an RBI single against the Florida Marlins in the first inning of a game in late May 2008.

Ryan Howard slides into third with a triple as Atlanta Braves third baseman Martin Prado looks for the throw in the sixth inning of a September game.

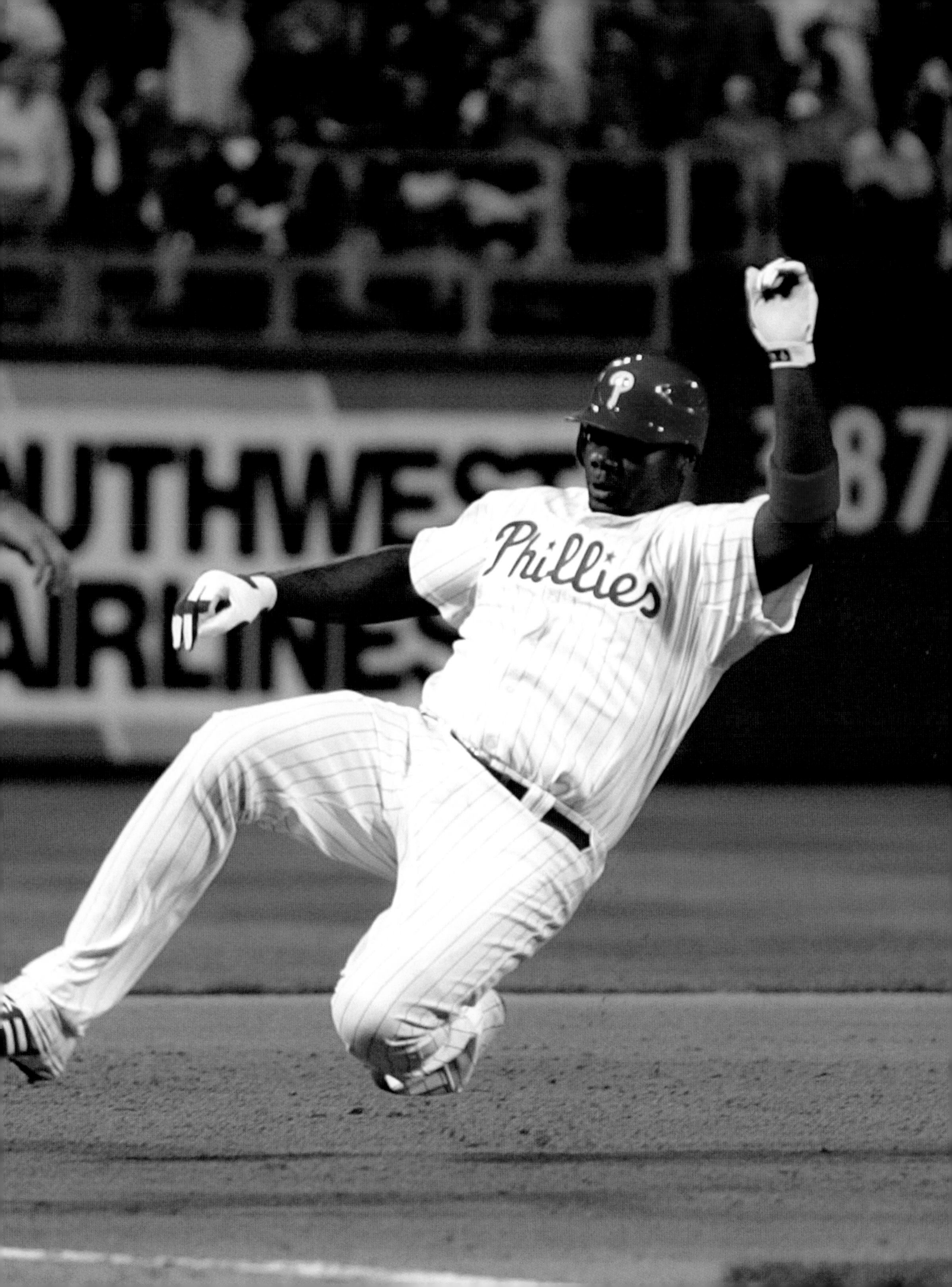
UTHWEST
ARLINES
Phillies

Season Stats

Pos	Player	Age	G	AB	R	H	2B	3B	HR	RBI	BB	SO	BA	OBP	SLG	SB	CS
C	Carlos Ruiz	29	117	320	47	70	14	0	4	31	44	38	.219	.320	.300	1	2
1B	Ryan Howard	28	162	610	105	153	26	4	48	146	81	199	.251	.339	.543	1	1
2B	Chase Utley	29	159	607	113	177	41	4	33	104	64	104	.292	.380	.535	14	2
3B	Pedro Feliz	33	133	425	43	106	19	2	14	58	33	54	.249	.302	.402	0	0
SS	Jimmy Rollins	29	137	556	76	154	38	9	11	59	58	55	.277	.349	.437	47	3
LF	Pat Burrell	31	157	536	74	134	33	3	33	86	102	136	.250	.367	.507	0	0
CF	Shane Victorino	27	146	570	102	167	30	8	14	58	45	69	.293	.352	.447	36	11
RF	Jayson Werth	29	134	418	73	114	16	3	24	67	57	119	.273	.363	.498	20	1
	Geoff Jenkins	33	115	293	27	72	16	0	9	29	24	68	.246	.301	.392	1	1
	Chris Coste	35	98	274	28	72	17	0	9	36	16	51	.263	.325	.423	0	1
	Greg Dobbs	29	128	226	30	68	14	1	9	40	11	40	.301	.333	.491	3	1
	Eric Bruntlett	30	120	212	37	46	9	1	2	15	21	35	.217	.297	.297	9	2
	So Taguchi	38	88	91	18	20	5	1	0	9	8	14	.220	.283	.297	3	0
	Matt Stairs	40	16	17	4	5	1	0	2	5	1	3	.294	.316	.706	0	0
	Mike Cervenak	31	10	13	0	2	0	0	0	1	0	5	.154	.154	.154	0	0
	Brad Harman	22	6	10	1	1	1	0	0	1	1	1	.100	.182	.200	0	0
	Tadahito Iguchi	33	4	7	0	2	1	0	0	0	0	0	.286	.286	.429	0	0
	Greg Golson	22	6	6	2	0	0	0	0	0	0	4	.000	.000	.000	1	0
	T.J. Bohn	28	14	5	1	2	1	0	0	3	0	1	.400	.400	.600	0	0
	Lou Marson	22	1	4	2	2	0	0	1	2	0	2	.500	.500	1.250	0	0
	Chris Snelling	26	4	4	1	2	1	0	1	1	1	0	.500	.500	1.500	0	0
	Andy Tracy	34	4	2	0	0	0	0	0	1	1	1	.000	.250	.000	0	0

Joe Blanton pitches in the first inning
against the St. Louis Cardinals in August
2008 in St. Louis.

NLDS Playoffs

When the Phillies capped yet another successful season by clinching their second consecutive playoff appearance, they knew that there was work to be done. The team still had a bad taste in its mouth following their three-game ouster from the 2007 NLDS by the Colorado Rockies. Their first-round opponents in 2008, the Milwaukee Brewers survived a late-season slump and a managerial change to earn a hard-fought playoff spot, their first post-season appearance since 1982.

The Brewers probably didn't know what to expect when the series opened up for the first two games in Philadelphia at Citizen's Bank Park. The sell-out crowd was enjoying post-season baseball for the second consecutive year after a 14-year hiatus. Expectations and the excitement level were high.

Game 1
Phillies 3, Brewers 1

The Phillies sent their ace in southpaw, Cole Hamels, to the mound for the opening game against the Brewers. Milwaukee countered with their fine right-hander Yovani Gallardo.

Hamels was masterful, using his outstanding change up to keep the Brewers off balance. The Phillies' supported him by putting up a three-spot in the home half of the third inning. Carlos Ruiz led off the inning with a single. He moved up a base when the Brewers muffed Hamels bunt attempt. Ever the clutch player, Chase Utley hit a line drive to center field just off the glove of Mike Cameron, scoring both Ruiz and Hamels. A pair of walks brought up Shane Victorino, who also drew base on balls to force in the third run of the game.

Hamels continued his mastery on the mound, pitching eight shutout innings in which he yielded just two hits and one walk; he also had nine strikeouts. With a 3-0 lead Phils Manager Charlie Manuel brought in Brad Lidge to close out the game. Lidge, who was 41 for 41 in save opportunities during the regular season, made it interesting in the ninth by giving up a run, but pitched out of a jam to preserve the first Phillies' playoff win since the 1993 World Series.

Unlike the 2007 playoffs in which they were swept, Philadelphia jumped on their opponent quickly and took a one game to none lead in the best-of-five series.

Cole Hamels bears down against a Milwaukee Brewers' batter during the first inning of Game 1 of the National League Division Series on October 1, 2008.

Members of the Phillies and Brewers are introduced prior
to the start during of Game 1 of the National League
Division Series on October 1, 2008, in Philadelphia.

Game 2
Phillies 5, Brewers 2

The resurgent one, right-hander Brett Myers, yielded a first-inning run to the Brewers in Game 2 and then settled down and pitched seven strong innings. Myers gave up only two hits, walked three, and struck out four. But perhaps the most important aspect of his game was an at-bat against Brewers ace C.C. Sabathia.

Trailing the Brewers 1–0, the Phillies offense went to work in the second inning. Pitching on just three days rest, Sabathia gave up hit to left field that Jayson Werth legged out for a double. Pedro Feliz doubled him home and the Phillies had tied the score at 1–1. With two outs, Myers hung in at the plate, fouling off pitches and finally drawing a walk. Jimmy Rollins also drew a free pass to load the bases. Down in the count against Sabathia, 1–2, The Flyin' Hawaiian Shane Victorino nailed the next pitch out of the park for a grand-slam home run, giving the Phillies a commanding 5–1 lead.

For all his inconsistency during the season, Myers pitched brilliantly the rest of the way before Brad Lidge came in to save the contest with a strong ninth inning.

The Phillies were now up two games to none in the best-of-five series. It also marked the first time that they enjoyed a 2-0 advantage in a playoff series since they lead the Kansas City Royals in the 1980 World Series.

(opposite) Shane Victorino follows his grand slam against the Brewers during the second inning of Game 2 of the National League Division Series on October 2, 2008. (above) Phillies fans wave towels before the start of Game 2 of the NLDS against the Milwaukee Brewers on October 2, 2008, in Philadelphia.

Game 3
Brewers 4, Phillies 1

With their backs against the wall, the Brewers returned to Milwaukee with a determination to get back in the series. Right-hander Dave Bush was outstanding, allowing the Phillies just a single run. And the Brewers were able to get an early lead against Jamie Moyer, who was not getting the strike calls he needed to be successful.

Mike Cameron and Bill Hall each drew walks in the bottom of the first, and each moved up a base when Moyer uncorked a wild pitch. With one out, Prince Fielder brought home Cameron with a sacrifice fly RBI, and then J.J. Hardy drove in Hall with a single. The Brewers led 2-0 after one.

They added another run in the fifth inning against reliever Clay Condrey. Cameron was hit by a pitch and moved to

third base on a single by Hall. Ryan Braun's sacrifice fly made it a 3-0 game.

The Phillies lone run came in the sixth inning when Jayson Werth tripled and scored on a Ryan Howard ground-out. Milwaukee added one more run in their half of the seventh and the Phillies just couldn't answer. Dave Bush pitched well and Salomon Torres got the save and it was a 2-1 series.

Game 4
Phillies 6, Brewers 2

With Joe Blanton pitching what could prove to be the deciding game of the series in Milwaukee, the Phillies wanted to give him an early lead. It didn't take long, as Jimmy Rollins led off the game with a homer against right-hander Jeff Suppan. It stayed a 1-0 contest until the Phils half of the third when they broke the game open.

With two men on base, Pat Burrell smacked a three-run blast into the seats in left field to give the Phillies a 4-0 lead. Before he had the chance to shake the hands of all his teammates in the dugout, Werth followed with a solo shot of his own, making it a 5-0 Phillies advantage.

Blanton breezed, pitching very well into the seventh inning. When he fell behind in the count against Prince Fielder hit and gave up a homer deep into the right-field seats to make it 6-1, Blanton's day was done. Ryan Madson relieved him and pitched two innings, giving up one run. And then Lidge came in and closed out the NLDS-winning game for the Phillies.

Next up were the Los Angeles Dodgers in the NLCS. ①

(opposite) Joe Blanton follows through on a pitch during the sixth inning of Game 4 of the National League Division Series on October 5, 2008, in Milwaukee. (above) Milwaukee Brewers manager Dale Sveum shakes hands with Charlie Manuel before first-inning action in Game 3 of the NLDS on October 4, 2008, in Milwaukee.

The Phillies celebrate after Game 4 of the National League Division Series, which they won 6–2, to advance to the National League Championship Series against the Los Angeles Dodgers.

NLDS Stats

Game 1 • October 1, 2008, at Citizens Bank Park

	1	2	3	4	5	6	7	8	9	R	H	E
Milwaukee Brewers	0	0	0	0	0	0	0	0	1	1	4	1
Philadelphia Phillies	0	0	3	0	0	0	0	0	x	3	4	1

PITCHERS: MIL - Gallardo, Stetter (5), Villanueva (5), Parra (8), Mota (8) • PHI - Hamels, Lidge (9) • WP - Cole Hamels LP - Yovani Gallardo • SAVE - Brad Lidge

HOME RUNS: MIL - none • PHI - none • **ATTENDANCE:** 45,929

Game 2 • October 2, 2008, at Citizens Bank Park

	1	2	3	4	5	6	7	8	9	R	H	E
Milwaukee Brewers	1	0	0	0	0	0	1	0	0	2	3	0
Philadelphia Phillies	0	5	0	0	0	0	0	0	x	5	9	1

PITCHERS: MIL - Sabathia, Stetter (4), McClung (5), Gagne (7), Torres (8) • PHI - Myers, Madson (8), Romero (8), Lidge (9) WP - Brett Myers • LP - C.C. Sabathia • SAVE - Brad Lidge

HOME RUNS: MIL - none • PHI - Victorino • **ATTENDANCE:** 46,208

Game 3 • October 4, 2008, at Miller Park

	1	2	3	4	5	6	7	8	9	R	H	E
Philadelphia Phillies	0	0	0	0	0	1	0	0	0	1	9	0
Milwaukee Brewers	2	0	0	0	1	0	1	0	x	4	11	0

PITCHERS: PHI - Moyer, Condrey (5), Durbin (6), Eyre (6), Madson (7) • MIL - Bush, Stetter (6), Villanueva (6), Gagne (8), Torres (9) • WP - David Bush • LP - Jamie Moyer • SAVE - Salomon Torres

HOME RUNS: PHI - none • MIL - none • **ATTENDANCE:** 43,992

Game 4 • October 5, 2008, at Miller Park

	1	2	3	4	5	6	7	8	9	R	H	E
Philadelphia Phillies	1	0	4	0	0	0	0	1	0	6	10	0
Milwaukee Brewers	0	0	0	0	0	0	1	1	0	2	8	0

PITCHERS: PHI - Blanton, Madson (7), Lidge (9) • MIL - Suppan, Gallardo (4), Parra (7), Mota (8) • WP - Joe Blanton LP - Jeff Suppan • SAVE - none

HOME RUNS: PHI - Burrell (2), Rollins, Werth • MIL - Fielder • **ATTENDANCE:** 43,934

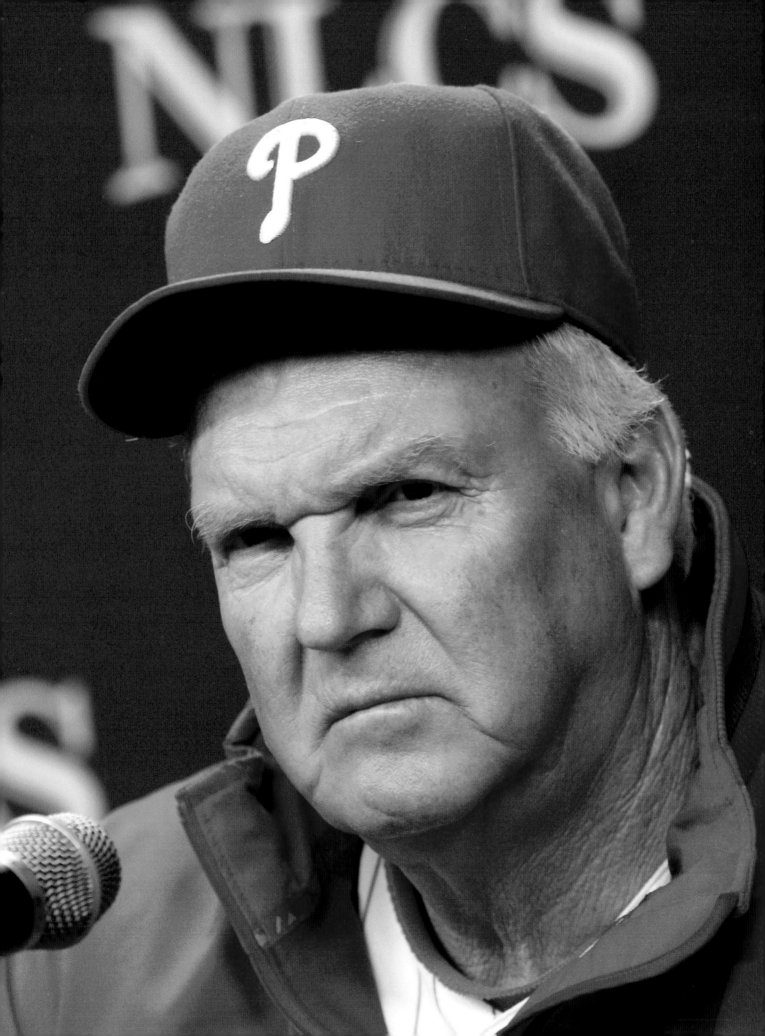

NLCS Playoffs

Fresh off the heels of their four-game victory over the Milwaukee Brewers in the NLDS, the Phillies prepared to take on the Los Angeles Dodgers for the right to represent the National League in the World Series. If they were ultimately successful, it would be Philadelphia's first trip to the Fall Classic since 1993. The Dodgers were trying to overcome their own two-decade World Series drought and were riding a wave of "MannyMania." New left fielder Manny Ramirez had engineered his escape from Boston and practically lifted the Dodgers on his broad shoulders and carried them into the post-season.

While Manny got most of the press and attention prior to the series, the Dodgers were a strong team with many other parts that made them click. But at the end of the day, if the Phillies could keep Manny from beating them, they knew they had a reasonably good chance to win the NLCS and return to the Fall Classic.

Game 1
Phillies 3, Dodgers 2

It didn't take long for the Los Angeles Dodger to quiet the normally boisterous crowd at Citizen's Bank Park in the first game of the NLCS. Veteran sinker/slider pitcher Derek Lowe managed to avoid the good part of the Phillies bats for the first five innings, completely controlling their high-powered offense.

At the same time, Phillies ace Cole Hamels spotted the Dodgers a pair of early runs. The first came in the first inning when the aforementioned Manny Ramirez barely missed a home run to the deepest part of the ballpark in center field and had to settle for a two-base hit that scored Andre Ethier. Later in the fourth stanza, Blake DeWitt hit a sacrifice fly that scored Matt Kemp to give the Dodgers a 2-0 advantage. The way that Lowe was controlling the Phillies, there was much concern in Philadelphia and good feelings in Los Angeles.

But in the sixth inning, Lowe began leaving his sinker up in the strike zone, a pitch that to some hitters looks like a hanging curve ball. The Phillies' bats came alive as Chase Utley hit a two run homer, and Pat Burrell followed with a solo shot to leap-frog the Dodgers and stake the Phillies to a 3-2 lead.

By then Hamels had righted himself and was untouchable. His night ended after seven innings in which he allowed six hits and two runs while striking out eight. Ryan Madson and Brad Lidge (by this point 44-for-44 in save opportunities) shut down the Dodgers for the last two innings and the Phillies led the best-of-seven series 1-0.

Charlie Manuel discusses strategy after Game 1 of the National League Championship Series against the Los Angeles Dodgers on October 9, 2008.

Jimmy Rollins kids around with the Dodgers' Manny Ramirez during batting

Pat Burrell smacks a home run in the sixth inning of Game 1 of the National League Championship Series.

Game 2
Phillies 8, Dodgers 5

Any time that Brett Myers is one of the offensive stars of a game, it's a pretty certain bet that the game in question was a wild one. And in NLCS Game 2 there was plenty of action, though most of it occurred in the first four innings.

The Dodgers took a 1–0 lead when Blake DeWitt grounded out to Ryan Howard to score Ethier in the top of the first inning. But the Phillies came back with a four spot in their half of the first against hard-throwing right hander Chad Billingsley. Carlos Ruiz and Myers both singled home runs before Shane Victorino added a two-run double to give the Phillies a 4–1 lead.

Los Angeles got a run back in the second on a James Loney single to score catcher Russell Martin. But in the bottom half of the inning, the Phillies added four more runs with key hits coming from Myers and Victorino.

Leading 8–2, the Phillies saw Manny Ramirez hit a three-run homer to left field to narrow the gap to 8–5, but after that Myers, Chad Durbin, J C. Romero, Ryan Madson, and Brad Lidge shut down the Dodgers offense, giving the Phillies a 2–0 series lead.

Game 3
Dodgers 7, Phillies 2

The series switched to Los Angeles where it was not without fireworks. The Dodgers immediately jumped on Phillies' starter Jamie Moyer, scoring five first-inning runs to to grab a 5–0 lead. Rafael Furcal, Andre Ethier, Manny

(opposite) Charlie Manuel holds the NLCS trophy after winning the National League Pennant on October 15, 2008, in Los Angeles. (above) Fans reach for a home run hit by Pat Burrell during sixth inning of Game 1 of the National League Championship Series.

Ramirez, and Casey Blake all singled before Blake DeWitt cleared the bases with a double to right field.

The Phillies answered back in the second when Ryan Howard led off the inning with a double and scored on a single by Pedro Feliz. But in the Dodger's half of the second, Furcal hit Moyer's first pitch into the stands for a 6-1 Dodger lead. The Phillies never mounted a comeback, but the benches cleared in the third inning when Dodgers starter Hiroki Kuroda threw a pitch over the head of Shane Victorino. Apparently the Dodgers felt that their hitters were being disrespected. In fact, Ramirez had seen a Brett Myers pitch sail behind his back in Game 2. But when this pitch went in the neighborhood of Victorino's head, he objected and the benches cleared. Ultimately, the fight had no impact on the outcome of the game, and the Dodgers were back in the series, trailing only two games to one.

Game 4
Phillies 7, Dodgers 5

The way this game progressed, with the Dodgers leading Philadelphia 5-3 after seven innings, it looked like Los Angeles was on track to even the series at two games each. Derek Lowe started for the Dodgers and gave them five decent innings in which he allowed the Phillies two runs on six hits. Phils starter Joe Blanton was touched for three runs in five innings.

But the eighth inning was when it all fell apart for the Dodgers. Reliever Cory Wade gave up a two-run homer to Shane Victorino that tied the game at five. Enter flame-throwing Dodger reliever Jonathan Broxton, who had yielded only two home runs in 69 innings during the regular season. Pinch hitter Matt Stairs hit an absolute blast deep into the stands in right field and the Phillies were leading 7-5.

After Blanton, the Phillies bullpen once again shut the Dodgers down. Scott Eyre, Ryan Madson, J.C. Romero, and Brad Lidge protected the two-run lead and as the game ended, the Phillies were up for the series 3-1.

Game 5
Phillies 5, Dodgers 1

With Cole Hamels facing Chad Billingsley, this game had all the earmarks of an old-time pitching duel. And while Hamels remained at the top of his game, the same could not be said of the young Los Angeles hurler. Jimmy Rollins homered to lead off the game and give the Phillies and Hamels a quick 1-0 lead.

In the third inning, Rollins started another good inning by leading off with a walk and stealing second. Chase Utley walked. RBI singles from Ryan Howard and Pat Burrell made it a 3-0 Phillies advantage.

With future Hall of Fame pitcher Greg Maddux on the mound for the Dodgers, the Phillies scored two more runs thanks to three errors made by shortstop Furcal. The only smudge on Cole Hamels record was a solo shot to Ramirez in the sixth inning. Manny did his part for Dodgers in the post-season, hitting .520 while accumulating four home runs, 10 RBIs, and 11 walks in eight playoff games.

But the story of the game—and maybe the series—was Cole Hamels, who pitched seven strong innings, followed again by Madson and Lidge. The Phillies won the game and the NLCS four games to one. They had secured their first trip to the World Series since 1993. ⓘ

Jayson Werth celebrates with teammates after Game 5 of the National League Championship Series on October 15, 2008, in Los Angeles. The Phillies won the game 5-1 to win the series.

NLCS Stats

Game 1 • October 9, 2008, at Citizens Bank Park

	1	2	3	4	5	6	7	8	9	R	H	E
Los Angeles Dodgers	1	0	0	1	0	0	0	0	0	2	7	1
Philadelphia Phillies	0	0	0	0	0	3	0	0	x	3	7	0

PITCHERS: LAD - Lowe, Park (6), Maddux (7), Kuo (8) • PHI - Hamels, Madson (8), Lidge (9) • WP - Cole Hamels
LP - Derek Lowe • SAVE - Brad Lidge
HOME RUNS: LAD - none • PHI - Burrell, Utley • **ATTENDANCE:** 45,839

Game 2 • October 10, 2008, at Citizens Bank Park

	1	2	3	4	5	6	7	8	9	R	H	E
Los Angeles Dodgers	0	1	1	3	0	0	0	0	0	5	8	1
Philadelphia Phillies	0	4	4	0	0	0	0	0	x	8	11	1

PITCHERS: LAD - Billingsley, Park (3), Beimel (3), McDonald (3), Kershaw (7), Wade (8) • PHI - Myers, Durbin (6),
Romero (7), Madson (7), Lidge (9) • WP - Brett Myers • LP - Chad Billingsley • SAVE - Brad Lidge
HOME RUNS: LAD - Ramirez • PHI - none • **ATTENDANCE:** 45,883

Game 3 • October 12, 2008, at Dodger Stadium

	1	2	3	4	5	6	7	8	9	R	H	E
Philadelphia Phillies	0	1	0	0	0	0	1	0	0	2	7	0
Los Angeles Dodgers	5	1	0	1	0	0	0	0	x	7	10	0

PITCHERS: PHI - Moyer, Condrey (2), Happ (3), Eyre (6), Durbin (7), Romero (8) • LAD - Kuroda, Wade (7), Broxton (9)
WP - Hiroki Kuroda • LP - Jamie Moyer • SAVE - none
HOME RUNS: PHI - none • LAD - Furcal • **ATTENDANCE:** 56,800

Game 4 • October 13, 2008, at Dodger Stadium

	1	2	3	4	5	6	7	8	9	R	H	E
Philadelphia Phillies	2	0	0	0	0	1	0	4	0	7	12	1
Los Angeles Dodgers	1	0	0	0	2	2	0	0	0	5	11	0

PITCHERS: PHI - Blanton, Durbin (6), Eyre (6), Madson (6), Romero (8), Lidge (8) • LAD - Lowe, Kershaw (6), Park (6), Beimel (6), Kuo (7), Wade (8), Broxton (8) • WP - Ryan Madson • LP - Cory Wade • SAVE - Brad Lidge

HOME RUNS: PHI - Stairs, Victorino • LAD - Blake • **ATTENDANCE:** 56,800

Game 5 • October 15, 2008, at Dodger Stadium

	1	2	3	4	5	6	7	8	9	R	H	E
Philadelphia Phillies	1	0	2	0	2	0	0	0	0	5	8	0
Los Angeles Dodgers	0	0	0	0	0	1	0	0	0	1	7	3

PITCHERS: PHI - Hamels, Madson (8), Lidge (9) • LAD - Billingsley, Park (3), Maddux (4), McDonald (6), Beimel (8), Wade (8), Kuo (9) • WP - Cole Hamels • LP - Chad Billingsley • SAVE - none

HOME RUNS: PHI - Rollins • LAD - Ramirez • **ATTENDANCE:** 56,800